OVERCOMING YOUR PROCRASTINATION

College Student Edition!

DR. LINDA SAPADIN

PsychWisdom Publishing

No More Guilt   No More Regrets
No More Excuse-Making

Formatting and Interior Design by Woven Red Author Services, www.WovenRed.ca

First Edition
ISBN: 978-0-9836766-4-5

The individuals described in this book are composites of several people. I have gone to great lengths to ensure that the actions, words and identities of individuals are disguised, yet remain true to the spirit of the story.

For additional resources, go to:
www.BeatProcrastinationCoach.com
www.PsychWisdom.com

For information about speaking engagements, TV and radio interviews, group sales and customized front page with logo, contact Dr. Sapadin at LSapadin@DrSapadin.com or 516 791-2780.

DEDICATED TO YOUR BEST SELF

Nurture it and Sustain it

Let it be Your Guide to a Fabulous Future

Table of Contents

INTRODUCTION

THIS IS WHERE
THE MAGIC WILL HAPPEN!

Smart and savvy you may be. Still your success in college won't be determined by your IQ but by what you do or don't do. This book will provide you with a ton of ideas on how to outsmart your procrastination - especially when the kid part of you wants to do nothing but play games, sleep, stay on your phone or hang with friends.

I'm a psychologist. If I could listen to you and hear exactly what your issues are, you'd be kicking butt right now! But I can't. So I wrote this book to help you be the best you can be. I won't lecture you, berate you, denigrate you nor give you any preachy advice. I'm not going to tell you what you *should* do but I am going to tell you what you *could* do. What you *could* do to have a fantastic and successful college experience!

My advice will be based on *your* personality style. Surely you know that people differ from one another in manner and mode. The greatest advice for one person may be absolutely wrong for another. For example, if your procrastination is fueled by a perpetual pursuit of *perfection*, you must pay *less* attention to details. Why? Because unless it's perfect, you'll feel the pressure to work on one more detail, one more detail, one more detail. No surprise you're driving yourself nuts and may be late handing in your paper! However, if your procrastination is fueled by a perpetual pursuit of *pie-in-the-sky dreams*, it's essential that you pay *more* attention to details. Why? Because if you don't attend to the details, your creative ideas will end up in the clouds – the real clouds!

But how am I going to know who you are so I can offer you the best ideas? Well, here's the fun part. You get to take a quiz – well, actually six quizzes - rank order them, then discover your highest ranking personality style. You'll Pass GO, collect $200 (only kidding) and focus on the chapter(s) dedicated to your style.

Rest assured, I do not desire to turn you into a no-fun study nerd. College years are definitely the time to have fun and sow your wild oats. Indeed, if you're straight and narrow now when you're young, when are you going to have a wild and crazy time? When you're middle aged? A senior citizen? I don't think so. I also have no wish to turn you into an "ideal" personality – even if I knew what that was. To do so would be counterproductive and rather insulting. Yes, it might be helpful if you were better organized like your sibling or less worried like your friend but you've got strengths they don't have. No need for a personality makeover. You already have many admirable traits.

My goal is simple. I want to help you develop the upgraded, enhanced version of YOU. I hope you want that too. I hope you're intrigued about acquiring valuable skills that will last you a lifetime. If you are, this is where the magic will happen. And I promise you, this book will *not* be TLTR (too long to read). Good ideas come in small packages.

Just one more thing before we move on. Surely you've noticed that many people babble on yet say nothing of substance while others use few words and hit the nail right on the head! I love those folks. That's why throughout this book, I'll be gifting you great quotes that I hope will inspire you. Ok, off we go!

"Though no one can go back and make a brand new start, anyone can start from now and make a brand new ending."
Carl Bard

CHAPTER 1

HOW TO OUTSMART YOUR PROCRASTINATION!

Do you even know why you're going to college? Perhaps you want to get that degree, launch an awesome career, even amaze the world with some brilliant achievement. But guess what? If you don't outsmart your propensity to procrastinate, your dreams are headed down that rabbit hole! Yup, of all the skills correlated with success, the ability to master your tendency to put things off is high on the list. Dragging your feet on needed work is like shooting yourself in the foot. Keep it up and sorry to say, it won't be just in the foot.

But what's wrong with wanting to make your life easy? Carpe diem; seize the day! Isn't that what college life is supposed to be about? Yes, you have a final exam in three weeks. And a research paper due in two weeks. Yes, you're ready to hit the books. But it's so easy to get distracted - parties to savor, sports events to attend, Instagrams to stalk, YouTube videos of adorable animals to watch. Now you're ready to do some serious studying. No big deal; you're just taking a short break to watch your favorite show. Then Oh My God! It's three hours later. Do you have time to get all your stuff done? Sure, if only you didn't need to do those pesky things like sleep, eat or attend classes.

Does this scenario sound familiar? Yes, the details of your story may differ but if the general theme hits home, stay with me. You'll learn how to fight your inertia and break out of routines that rip your self-esteem apart. Are you pumped up yet? I hope so! I don't promise it'll be a snap of the fingers to change ingrained habits. But I do promise that it won't be as hard as you think as I'll be offering you advice for your personality style that fits like a glove.

3 Procrastinators Walk into a Bar

Yup, procrastination is the butt of many a joke. No problem with that…until it gets to be no laughing matter! People aren't perfect. We put things off. We forget. We don't *feel* like doing it. Your room remains a mess even though you promised yourself you'd clean it up. You were going to study this morning but Snapchat robbed you of the time. No big deal. But when procrastination is not just an occasional occurrence but is *chronic and pervasive*, it *is* a big deal! It'll sabotage your success in college and beyond. So, it's crucial to address it NOW!

You're probably aware that there's a big difference between being angry on occasion and being an angry person. But do you know that there's a big difference between procrastinating on occasion and being a chronic procrastinator? If you're wondering how extensive your procrastination pattern is, answer these 10 questions. Respond "YES" if you *often* do what's described, "NO" if you *rarely or never* do it:

1. Do I find that a quick break like checking Instagram can end studying for hours?
2. Do I have study sessions with friends that turn into talk about that new bar in town?
3. Do I have trouble finishing assignments because I believe they still need more work?
4. Do I leave assignments unfinished, jumping from one to another without completing any?
5. Do I worry about getting my stuff done on time but somehow my worry doesn't turn into action?
6. Do I have a habit of pulling all-nighters to get my work done?
7. Do I justify my procrastination with excuses like: "I forgot" or "this task is dumb?"
8. Do I tend to say 'yes' to what others want, then have no time for my own work?
9. Do I believe I have great ideas but find it hard to do all the details that would bring those ideas to fruition?
10. Do I enjoy discussing symbolism in contemporary works - like Avenger movies - but can't get motivated to do the same for assignments - like Shakespeare's plays?

How many "YES" answers did you have? If it's a lot, I'm impressed. You've found so many ways to procrastinate. But beware! There's trouble ahead if you keep telling yourself "I'll do it later" - then later you slip into something more comfortable like umm - a coma.

Still with me? Awesome! I've got important things to tell you before you take the quizzes.

"To Do or Not to Do?"

What exactly is procrastination? It's not just laziness as many believe. It's an approach-avoidance conflict. Part of you knows you need (or even want) to do a task but another part of you resists making the time and effort to do it. Like Hamlet, you're torn between two impulses: *"to do or not to do."* This ambivalence makes it tough for you to take action. So what happens?

You may begin to tackle the task yet lingering resistance results in your working at a snail's pace. Or you may stay stuck until the last possible moment when you lurch into action, prodded on by an impending deadline or a ticked-off third party. Or you may work non-stop but you're so fixated on perfection that you don't finish your masterpiece on time. Stuck in your crippling conflict, your energy remains damned - damning you to yet another frustrating setback.

Some students blame their procrastination on a lazy gene. Yet, far from being sluggards as the stereotype would have it, most students have an abundance of energy for what they *want* to do. But when it comes to what they're *expected* to do, their energy dissipates. Are you one of those students? Perhaps you feel that boring assignments are devoid of meaning; they turn you off, frustrate you. You may feel angry, annoyed. Is reading this stuff relevant to your life? Will it get you a better job? You doubt it. College feels like a waiting game – just putting in your time until you graduate.

If you believe your procrastination is a sign of disinterest, here are two things to keep in mind:

- Discover who the most passionate professors are and enroll in their classes, even if the subject matter is not initially appealing to you. An exciting teacher can make a calculus course fascinating while a boring teacher can make a human sexuality course a drag.
- Appreciate that life requires you to engage in some learning that you dislike in order to get to where you want to be. Read that sentence once more. Imprint it on your brain. It's an important life lesson.

Still, you may wonder - why can't I live in the moment doing only what I feel like doing? Because a funny thing happens when professors give you an assignment. They expect you to do it! And if you don't or you do a half-assed job, stuff happens. Bad stuff!

So what's the goal? In one word: *balance*. And if there's one thing that will throw you off balance, it's procrastination. Yes, it's tough to maintain a balanced life between what you *want* to do and what you *need* to do, particularly for your generation. No other generation has lived in a world that provides so many cheap and easily accessible distractions: websites, blogs,

Pinterest, Instagram, Twitter, YouTube, Podcasts, video games, chat rooms, texting and the list goes on. Plus, if you're living away from home, no longer do your parents function as watchdogs encouraging you to take care of your responsibilities, admonishing you to stay on track.

Does that mean you're doomed to be seduced by surrounding distractions? Absolutely not! You can break the pattern. Indeed, you *need* to break the pattern. Procrastinate in adult life and the consequences are more severe, not less. You're hired for a dream job only to be let go when they notice your less than sparkling work habits. You keep putting off paying bills; now the collection agency is on your back. You promised yourself you'd revise your resume but never did; no surprise, you're still stuck in that soul-sucking, dead-end job.

Yup, procrastination can have many unforeseen effects. So, I'm delighted you're learning how to squash it before it squashes your future.

You've Got Company!

More than 50% of students who start a degree program don't complete it! And that number keeps inching up. The primary reasons students don't finish: failure to assess priorities, finish projects, deal with distractions, maintain self-discipline, stay emotionally engaged, feel empowered. These are all key elements of procrastination. So, is dropping out of school in the cards for you? If it is, this could be good news or bad news.

First the good: If you're the next Steve Jobs or Bill Gates, go ahead and drop out. College may actually be holding you back. You're one of those rare people who wake up each morning exuberant about work. You've got a sense of purpose. Your creativity is humming. Your curiosity is buzzing. You're engaged – with inspiring ideas, electrifying energy!

Now the bad: Chances are you're *not* the next Steve Jobs or Bill Gates. Dropping out of school may be quitting on your future. In today's tough economic climate, a college education is a prerequisite for many careers. If you decide to drop out of one educational program to enter another that's more to your liking, it may be a good idea. But if you're simply dropping out, make sure you know what you're dropping into. Don't let it be unemployment or underemployment.

Put Your Butt Where it Belongs

Will Rogers, born in 1879, was a Cherokee Indian, a cowboy, a movie star, a columnist and finally a legend. He was one smart guy but no boring intellectual. He spoke in simple words that everyone could understand: *"Even if you're on the right track, you'll get run over if you just sit there."*

Are you on the right track just sitting there? Or on the wrong track where your butt doesn't belong? Maybe college *is not* the best place for you, yet you'd thrive in an apprenticeship or vocational training program better suited to your interests and inclinations. Or, maybe college *is* the best place for you, yet you're in the business school when your true interest lies in the arts. Or, you're in a college where the atmosphere is stifling, yet you're certain you'll thrive in a college with a more relaxed ambiance. Hence, give serious thought to whether you're in the wrong place.

If your answer is yes, consider making a change. If you wish to learn a marketable trade or a valuable skill, go for it! There'll always be a need for auto mechanics, electricians, carpenters, roofers, beauticians, appliance repair people and a host of other positions that will always be in demand. Indeed, if you're eager to learn a valuable "blue-collar" skill, you may very well do better – financially and emotionally – than peers who finish college but still have no idea about what they want to do and no marketable skill.

> *"Ask yourself what makes you come alive and go do that, because what the world needs is people who have come alive."*
> **Howard Thurman**

Then again, maybe you're on the right track but sitting there doing squat. If that's true, it's time to learn what's holding you back. Here are a few possibilities:

You procrastinate - even when you don't want to.

This is termed *perceived helplessness,* which leaves you with a lingering sense of powerlessness. You may direct this feeling *inward,* viewing yourself as stupid or incompetent. Or *outward,* feeling anger toward others or toward the program you're in.

You rationalize your procrastination, telling yourself you can't do anything about it.

You shrug it off saying, *"I'm just lazy by nature."* Or, you make self-vindicating excuses saying, *"I have a crappy memory."* Or, you forestall criticism by joking or boasting about your failures and fiascos, glossing over the problems it creates for you now and in your future.

You start off on the right track, yet get easily sidelined with more magnetic affairs.

Yes, intense work can be intimidating. As you delve into a task, you may find yourself baffled, bewildered. Rather than staying with the work or seeking assistance, you distract yourself with easier, more enjoyable tasks like posting on your social media accounts.

You experience recurring regret which eats away at your self-confidence.

You may literally feel this regret building as the moment of truth draws closer - a frightening feeling that can either reinforce your inertia or finally get you moving to do what you need to do.

"Regrets, I've had a few, too few to mention," crooned Sinatra. If your regrets are truly too few to mention, great! However, if you continue dawdling and delaying, I guarantee your regrets will be too many to mention. Over time, these regrets will close windows of opportunity and you'll end up fulfilling a shell of your potential. Three examples:

David's Story

David used to brag about making his first million before he turned 30. But now he's losing faith in himself. Watching his friends earn high grades while he's struggling to finish his incompletes is not a recipe for success. His worries are justified. Though he's just as smart as his friends, a casual approach to responsibilities means he won't graduate on time. David's learning an important lesson the hard way: no matter how high your potential is, if you don't *activate* that potential by *doing,* you become less competent as time marches on.

Jason's Story

Jason gets easily distracted with whatever, until the night before his paper is due. Then ideas suddenly pop into his head. He gets focused and works right through the night; then victory! Except when there's a glitch. Then, he relies on a Hail Mary, making up one excuse after another as to why his assignment is late, praying for a reprieve from a kind-hearted professor. Piss-poor strategy Jason. Football coaches call for a Hail Mary only when time is running out and they're out of options. Not the best way to approach your studies as *a Hail Mary typically fails in the stadium as well as the classroom.*

Maria's Story

Maria knew for months that she had what she called *"a funny spot"* on her skin. She was so nervous about it that she only told her best friend who encouraged her to get it checked out at the health clinic. Instead, Maria went to WebMD where she read about what her symptoms might mean, scaring herself into doing nothing. Tragically, something was wrong. By the time she saw a doctor, her cancer was pretty far advanced. Maria regrets what she calls her "stupidity." She knows her behavior made no sense yet it's not unusual for procrastinators to let *emotion trump reason.*

Though procrastination rarely results in such dire consequences, lots of smaller regrets take their toll. So, I hope you take steps to ensure that you're on the right track and not just sitting there doing nothing.

Discover Your "BUT!"

Still with me? Excellent, as I'd like to share a story with you. My first book on procrastination I wanted to title **"Discover Your But!"** My publisher said nope; people might misinterpret it as **"Discover Your Butt!"** Seriously? Yup, seriously!

Hence the title became **"It's About Time!"** A thoughtful title, still I like my *"But!"* Here's why. *"But"* is a word procrastinators use *a lot* to justify why they didn't do something, as in:

- "I was going to take care of it *but......*"
- "I wanted to study *but.....*"
- "I expected to be on time *but....*"

The most valuable thing you need to know about "but" is this:

> *What follows "BUT" is the essence of the communication.*
> *What precedes "BUT" simply softens the blow.*

Intuitively, you already know this. If a professor tells you, *"You wrote a good report but..."* you brace yourself for criticism. If your date says to you, "You're a terrific person *but..."* you prepare yourself for rejection. Though you can't control what others say to you, you can control what you say to yourself. Hence, do yourself a great big favor and place *the action-oriented* part of your message *after* the *"but."* An example: "I'd like to join you *but I need to finish my report first."*

Neglect to do so and this 3-letter word will be your never-ending excuse as to why you didn't do what you were going to do. *"But I'm too tired; but I was too busy; but I forgot; but, but, but..."* Clearly, you've got to figure out a way to get the better of your buts, which is why I've written this book. Stay with me and I'll provide you with the tools to do just that!

Oh, one more thing about 3-letter words. You now know that procrastinators often use *"but"* to *sabotage* their success. Do you know that there's another 3-letter word that can *ensure* your success? The word is *"and."* So simple yet so powerful.

"And" makes connections; *but"* cancels out connections. Notice the difference between these two sentences?

- I was going to finish this report *but* sure I'll join you. (Oops, there goes any work you were going to do.)
- I need to finish my report *and* I'll join you when I'm done. (You recognize that both work and fun are important; simple but profound difference.)

Good-bye Negativity!

As you outsmart your procrastination, you'll not only be saying good-bye to your "buts," you'll also be saying good-bye to some not-so-nice emotions.

Panic and Anxiety

I call this the *"Oh, my God!"* syndrome. You panic about whether you can do the work, whether you'll go loco over your lackluster grades or whether you'll fall so far behind that you won't *ever* be able to catch up. Even if you do catch up, you taste the bitter residue of anxiety as you agonize over the quality of your work, your capabilities and your future.

Feeling Discouraged

In contrast to the red-hot frenzy of panic, feeling discouraged is the desolate, disheartening ebb emotion. Upset with yourself, you may be tempted to give up. It feels like it's all too much! Harboring a negative mindset is like swimming against the current. It makes everything harder. You expend so much energy, yet you don't get very far. You might deflect your negativity outward, finding fault with others. Or inward, finding fault with yourself. Want to stop riding the roller coaster of hysterical highs and discouraging lows? Keep reading; I've got lots of ideas for you!

Feeling Depressed

Depression is physically and spiritually crushing. You keep hoping something good will happen only to be let down once again, leaving you with strong feelings of helplessness and hopelessness. *I can't do it; No use even trying; I may as well give up* are typical thoughts of depressed students. Anyone can have down moments. If talking with friends or getting a good night's sleep revives your energy, there may not be much to worry about. But if your depression lingers, **don't ignore it!** It may be that procrastination is the trigger for your depression or that depression is the trigger for your procrastination. Either way, I strongly urge you to start therapy to learn skills that will help you reduce or even end your depression.

Denial

Some students defend their procrastination by calling it "creative." It's good to procrastinate, they claim. Why do things early when you can do them later? When denial is at the helm, people can fool themselves about almost anything. If you're tempted to spin your procrastination into a laudable trait, think again. If there's one thing you owe yourself, it's honesty!

Good Reasons to Put Things Off

But aren't there *ever* good reasons to put things off? Absolutely! Here are three excellent ones:

You're Overcommitted

You already have so many things on your plate, you can't tackle one more task and do it justice. In such a situation, it's good to be open about your predicament - both with yourself and others. Rather than simply procrastinate (say you'll do it, but don't), create a time in the near future when you won't be spread so thin. At that point, you'll be better able to focus on your work.

You're Overly Emotional

People often regret what they've done in the heat of anger, hurt, despair, fear, even joy. If your feelings are over the top, it's usually a good idea to postpone making a decision or tackling a tough task. When your emotions cool down, you'll be better able to consult both your head and your heart and then decide what to do.

You're Impulsive

We're a fast-paced society. We're impatient. We want things to be done, fixed, completed right away. The more technologically sophisticated we are, the faster we expect things to happen. Act impulsively, however, and you may regret those actions. So, if you've got a spur-of-the-moment idea about how to handle an assignment, take time to think it through before you commit to doing it that way.

Excited yet about changing your life for the better? I hope so. Now, off we go to quiz land!

"The self is not something ready-made,
but something in continuous formation through choice of action."
~ **John Dewey**

CHAPTER 2

WHAT'S YOUR PERSONALITY STYLE?
6 QUIZZES

Raise your hand if you want to learn more about WHO YOU ARE?

Excellent!

Looks like you're ready to get valuable and entertaining insights about none other than – yourself!

That's so important, as "the only thing more expensive than education is ignorance." Those are not my words. They are the words of none other than the illustrious **Ben Franklin.**

Style 1

For each question, write down the number that best describes *you*.
1 = Not typically me 2 = Sometimes that's me
3 = Yup, that's often me!

Quiz # 1	1, 2 or 3
1. Do I have a black or white mentality, paying scant attention to the gray area in between?	
2. Do I berate myself for falling short when my own high standards haven't been met?	
3. Have others told me I'm being too harsh on myself; ease up?	
4. Do I give a great deal of importance to details others overlook or view as no big deal?	
5. Do I spend too much time on my assignments, trying to make them as good as they could possibly be?	
6. Do I tend to berate myself for what I "should" or "shouldn't" have done?	
7. Am I satisfied with what I did only if it's as good as it could possibly be?	
8. Do I view my failures as embarrassments that I'd like to keep secret?	
9. Do I have difficulty maintaining my sense of humor while struggling to do a tough task?	
10. With group projects, do I take over more than my fair share of responsibilities to ensure that the project is done right?	
TOTAL SCORE for STYLE 1	

Style 2

1 = Not typically me 2 = Sometimes that's me
3 = Yup, that's often me!

Quiz # 2	1, 2 or 3
1. Do I wait for opportunities to drop in my lap rather than take an active, "go get 'em" approach?	
2. Do I think a lot about what I'd like to accomplish but find it tough to get projects off the ground?	
3. Do I let time drift by with passive activities like watching TV, scrolling through Instagram or daydreaming?	
4. Do I find it tough to carry out the routines and responsibilities others expect from me?	
5. Do I long to go from 'A to Z' without dealing with those dismal details in between?	
6. Do I wish someone else would handle the annoying details of life, freeing me up to be more creative?	
7. Do I have a habit of beginning my sentences with, "I'll try to . . ." or "I wish . . ."?	
8. Have others accused me of having my head in the clouds, neglecting to focus on what needs to be done now?	
9. Do I tend to live in the moment, putting previous plans and priorities on the back burner?	
10. Do I expect myself to achieve great things but wonder why they're not happening?	
TOTAL SCORE for STYLE 2	

Style 3

1 = Not typically me 2 = Sometimes that's me
3 = Yup, that's often me!

Quiz # 3	1, 2 or 3
1. Do I hesitate to leave my comfort zone, wanting to avoid whatever will make me feel anxious?	
2. Do I slow myself down before working on a project by worrying about the "what ifs"?	
3. Do I have difficulty making decisions, frequently vacillating about what to do?	
4. Do I often say or think, "I can't..." or "I don't know how to..."?	
5. Do I feel nervous about whether I can accomplish what's expected of me?	
6. Do I become flustered when an unexpected event disrupts my routine?	
7. Do I get easily agitated thinking that I may be doing an assignment the wrong way?	
8. Do I maximize the challenges I face (making them bigger than they really are), and minimize my ability to deal with them?	
9. Do I look for reassurance from others before I can begin to work on an assignment?	
10. When faced with a challenging task, do I wish someone would take me by the hand and show me the way?	
TOTAL SCORE for STYLE 3	

Style 4

1 = Not typically me 2 = Sometimes that's me
3 = Yup, that's often me!

Quiz # 4	1, 2 or 3
1. Do I ignore my assignments, then at the last minute work frantically to get them done?	
2. Does my motivation to do my work change quickly and dramatically?	
3. Am I easily seduced into responding to the need of the moment?	
4. Does my life feel like it's one repetitive crisis after another?	
5. Do I act in ways that others find provocative or attention-getting?	
6. Do I feel that my life is a whirlwind; I'm never quite sure what the next day will bring?	
7. Do I enjoy taking risks and living on the edge?	
8. Do I start doing a task, then abruptly move on to something else?	
9. Does my life seem so dramatic, it could be made into a reality show or soap opera?	
10. Do I have little patience for slow, detail-oriented tasks, preferring quick, action-oriented ones?	
TOTAL SCORE for STYLE 4	

Style 5

1 = Not typically me 2 = Sometimes that's me
3 = Yup, that's often me!

Quiz # 5	1, 2 or 3
1. Do I blow off tasks I'm expected to do, claiming I've forgotten them or that they're unimportant?	
2. Do I become sulky, sarcastic, or argumentative when asked to do something I don't want to do?	
3. Do I take offense when others tell me how I should do things differently?	
4. Do I feel that others make unreasonable demands on me?	
5. Do I tend to criticize or ridicule people in authority?	
6. When others ask me to do a chore, do I feel like they're hassling or nagging me?	
7. Do I believe that I'm doing a better job than others think I'm doing?	
8. Do I feel resentful when asked to do a task for someone else?	
9. Do others get annoyed with me for failing to do my share of the work in a timely way?	
10. Do I sabotage tasks I dislike doing by working slowly or ineffectively?	
TOTAL SCORE for STYLE 5	

Style 6

1 = Not typically me 2 = Sometimes that's me
3 = Yup, that's often me!

Quiz # 6	1, 2 or 3
1. Is it tough for me to say "no" to others?	
2. Do I find it hard to honor my own priorities when others want me to do something else?	
3. When I'm doing a task for another, do I wonder, "How did I get into this?"	
4. Do I run around doing a lot, yet don't get to what I really want or need to do?	
5. Do I have a strong need for approval from others?	
6. Do I hate to ask others for help, afraid of bothering or inconveniencing them?	
7. Do I get over-involved with other people's problems, postponing attention to my own?	
8. Do I have trouble setting limits with others who want me to be there for them?	
9. Do I feel bewildered that I don't have enough time to do what I need to do?	
10. Do I enjoy being busy, but secretly think that maybe I don't know any other way to be?	
TOTAL SCORE for STYLE 6	

Drum Roll Please.... Time for the Results!

Did you find the quizzes thought-provoking? Did you enjoy taking them? If you're shaking your head "yes," consider sharing them with your friends. It's always fun to discover how we differ in personality styles. Now, the results! Write your individual quiz score in the Total Score box. Then, rank order your styles.

PERSONALITY STYLE	TOTAL SCORE	RANK ORDER
Style 1. Perfectionist		
Style 2. Dreamer		
Style 3. Worrier		
Style 4. Crisis-Maker		
Style 5. Defier		
Style 6. Pleaser		

Any surprises? You may be startled by the results or the quizzes may have simply reinforced what you already knew. If you scored high on several styles, don't panic! You're *not* a hopeless case. These are all *normal* human traits. And we're all human (unless Alexa's reading this now).

Each style is indicative of the *outer polarities* of one of these traits.

- **Attention to Details:** The perfectionist pays *too much* attention to details - the dreamer *doesn't pay enough* attention.
- **Focus on Fears:** The worrier's *overly concerned* with what might happen if... - the crisis-maker *isn't sufficiently concerned* until the 11th hour.
- **Relationship to Others:** The defier goes *against* what others want - the pleaser is *overly oriented* toward what others want.

Nothing wrong with these traits, it's just best to be more centrist. For example, if on the perfectionist scale you score mostly 9 or 10s, you've got trouble! If you score 7 or 8s, no problem – you're flexible, able to adapt to changing conditions instead of being rigid and unbending.

Here's a brief description of each style - with its hallmark "BUT" excuse. You'll learn more about each one when you delve into the chapter dedicated to it.

1. The Perfectionist: "... BUT it's got to be perfect!"

As a perfectionist, you find it tough to complete a task because you don't want to do anything less than a perfect job. You may worry about satisfying your own high standards or satisfying the high expectations others have of you. Once you've started a task, you may spend far more time and energy on it than is needed. Overworking, paradoxically, is an unrecognized form of procrastination. Though you're working hard, you're not working smart.

2. The Dreamer: "... BUT I hate doing all those dismal details!"

As a dreamer, you wish you could go from A to Z without having to deal with all those details in between. Though you relish creative ideas, you fall short on doing the work that's needed to bring those ideas to fruition. You may be adept at championing big plans yet often those plans go nowhere, disappointing you once again. Soaring thinking without ground level doing is a prescription for becoming disenchanted with school, disheartened with ever attaining your dreams.

3. The Worrier: "... BUT what if I make the wrong choice?"

As a worrier, you proceed through life with caution, worrying about your future and what might happen if…. Maximizing problems while minimizing your ability to deal with them will leave you feeling agitated and anxious. It's tough to make decisions when you're never quite sure what to do. And even after you've made a decision, you worry whether it was the right one. Oh, if only there weren't so many choices to make!

4. The Crisis-Maker: "... BUT I work best under pressure!"

As a crisis-maker, you crave living on the edge. Addicted to the rush of high emotion, imminent danger and emergency action, you wait until the final moment to move into gear. Though a last minute crisis can be exhausting, it can also be exhilarating - an adventure, even a pathway to proving yourself a hero. Pulling all-nighters may be your style; yet in those quiet moments of self-reflection you wonder how much easier life would be if only you gave yourself more time to do what you need to do.

5. The Defier: "... BUT why should I do it?"

As a defier, you may be openly rebellious, passive-aggressive or a combination of the two. If you're openly rebellious, you directly defy authority. By procrastinating, you set your own idiosyncratic time schedule - one that nobody else can control. If you're passive-aggressive, you're not blatant with your defiance; you simply say you'll do it, but you don't. Whichever type of defier you are, you view many obligations, even routine tasks (like attending class or studying for exams) as impositions on your time.

6. The Pleaser: "... BUT I can't say "No!"

As a pleaser, your own needs often end up at the bottom of the pile as you're constantly saying "yes" to others. With so much on your plate, you frequently feel frazzled by the lack of time, frenzied with your countless commitments. You haven't yet mastered the art of creating priorities, setting limits, and deciding for yourself what you'll do and when to do it - which means you're a prime candidate for early burnout!

6 Personality Styles

Personality Style	Thinking Style	Speaking Style	Acting Style
Perfectionist	Either/Or	I should…	Impeccable
Dreamer	Vague	I wish…	Passive
Worrier	Anxious	What if…?	Cautious
Crisis-Maker	Impulsive	Don't feel like it…	Dramatic
Defier	Challenging	Why should I…?	Oppositional
Pleaser	Dutiful	Sure, no problem!	Agreeable

You'll soon be delving into the chapters dedicated to your personality styles. But first, time for a commercial. Just kidding! It's time to learn about the *process* of change.

You know people don't change overnight. And they certainly don't change just because someone else wants them to. No, it's an ongoing process. To quicken your road to success, the next chapter will explain how it happens.

CHAPTER 3

CHANGE:
HOW IS THE KEY!

Amazing things can happen when you view change as an opportunity to grow instead of shrugging your shoulders and saying *"I can't!"* Yes, it's hard to change ingrained patterns. And it takes time. You may become impatient with yourself. Others may become impatient with you, imploring you to *"just do it!"*

Oh, how I hate the word *"just"* when it pertains to change. We don't change *"just"* because someone wants us to - even when we ourselves want to. But, please don't swing the pendulum in the opposite direction. Chase away those demons that tell you, "you can't change; it's too hard; it's not in your DNA." Such a mindset will sabotage your efforts before you even begin.

Though it's true "you are who you are," that doesn't mean you can't alter your habits to become a better you! Indeed, if you don't confront your demons now, I guarantee they will confront *you* as time marches on. So, be open to changing habits that are not serving you well. Change won't happen with a snap of your fingers. It's a *process* that begins with awakening.

Awakening

If you're living your life in a daze, refusing to take responsibility for your actions or non-actions, change won't be in the cards. This may seem obvious, but it's not to everyone. Lots of people are in denial. Their take on the matter:

- What problem? - It's **your** problem. - Leave me alone!
- Stop picking on me! - Why does this always happen to me?

Or, they may admit that they procrastinate but they:
- Laugh it off, no big deal!
- Project the problem onto *something* else: "Lousy luck; tough timing."
- Project the problem onto *someone* else: "They don't understand; they're so unfair!"

Awakening is a prerequisite for change. If you're still reading, you've passed the stage of awakening. Woo-hoo! But it's only the first step. What's next?

Awareness

You're aware of the hassles you create for yourself. You want to change. No problem now, right? Wish I could tell you that's true but the truth is there's still a bumpy road ahead of you that can derail your progress.

Blame it on your brain that bombards you with competing messages. The *executive part* of your brain wants you to buckle down and do what needs to be done in a timely manner. But the *emotional part* of your brain doesn't want to be bothered. Both parts are in a wrestling match, fighting to be head honcho. Who wins?

If it's your emotional self, you've got problems; no wonder you're behind in your work. But if it's your executive self, you've also got problems. You don't want to become Mr. Spock, that icon of rationality, do you? So, what's the answer? *Both parts of your brain need to work cooperatively,* making sure each one has sufficient time in the sun. Do this and you'll take a quantum leap forward in conquering your procrastination!

Commitment

Oh, the futility of good intentions! Sure, you want to change but are you ready to make a *no-nonsense commitment to change* - despite the roadblocks you'll encounter? In your quiet moment of truth, when you're alone and not under pressure by anyone, can you - *your executive self in harmony with your emotional self* - make a solemn pledge to change?

You know it won't be easy. Yet, you're open to persevering and persisting. You know *why* you want to change; you know *who* you want to be; you know the *life* you want to live. You know that in order to make it happen, your actions must adhere to your beliefs. You have a vision in your mind; you have the will to do what it takes. You're tired of disappointing yourself; you're fed up with feeling frustrated. You're ready to get off your *butt;* banish your *buts* and make it happen!

When the student is ready, the master will appear. This is not only Zen philosophy; this is appreciating the power of the committed mind.

How?

You've made a serious commitment to change. But *how* will you do it? The old is so familiar. And the new? Well, you're not quite comfortable with it, especially when you hear people telling you what you *must* do. You *must* get up early, start studying right away, never miss a class, spend weekends in the library, put mega time into research and don't forget about working out, eating right and doing volunteer work. Don't procrastinate on any of these matters!

Sure, that's all possible. But I prefer to offer you advice that takes into account that you're a person, not a robot. I want to show you ways to change that meshes *with* your personality style, so you don't have to turn yourself inside out to outsmart your procrastination. I can't make you be successful but I can provide you with the skills you'll need to achieve success. After that, it's up to you!

Success!

You've not only learned the skills, you've *applied* the skills. You've triumphed over your procrastination! You've developed a new mindset and new habits. And the best part is that you haven't become a no-fun dreary workaholic. Quite the opposite. Life has become easier, not harder; more fun, not less fun.

How could this be? The answer is obvious (once you hear it). It's because everything is more difficult when you do it reluctantly. Scratch the griping and grumbling and your work becomes *easier* to do! No more guilt, no more regrets, no more excuse-making. I hope I've sold you on the idea of freeing yourself from the spell of procrastination. For once you do, there'll be no stopping you!

Just a Few More Things

In a moment, you'll head straight to the chapter dedicated to your highest scoring style. What about the other chapters? Should you read them too? It's not a *should*; it's a *could*. You'll definitely learn new skills, so unless your eyes are glazing over, do it. And don't forget to read the very last chapter which has a whole lot of goodies for *all* personality styles.

Soon you'll meet fellow students with the same issues as you. You'll learn *thinking skills* to get you moving, *speaking skills* to create a new narrative and *action strategies* to get you going! To top it off, there'll be a *guided imagery* to tap your creative mind. You may be surprised to learn that I've not written a section for altering your feelings. Want to take a guess why?

Figured it out? Feelings are highly resistant to deliberate modification. A friend tells you to be happy but you're bummed out. Do you alter your emotions just because *she* wants you to? Or even because *you* want to? Oh, if only it were that simple! This doesn't mean you have no control over your emotions; it just means that the indirect approach works best.

"Happiness is as a butterfly
which when pursued is always beyond our grasp,
but which if you will sit down quietly, may alight upon you."
Nathaniel Hawthorne.

"Happiness is a warm puppy."
Charles Schulz (creator of Peanuts)

Get the idea? When you're doing what you like, being with people or puppies you enjoy, happiness may alight upon you. But *force* yourself to be happy when you're not and it simply doesn't work. I'm betting that happiness will be your luscious dessert when you implement the ideas in this book.

Let's Do This!

CHAPTER 4

THE PERFECTIONIST
...BUT IT'S GOT TO BE PERFECT!

Welcome Perfectionists! You have many exceptional qualities. You're hard-working and industrious. You set high standards for yourself. You're attentive to the details. You're always looking for ways to improve what you do. So, what's wrong with trying to be perfect?

It may sound strange, but perfectionism could be fueling your procrastination. No matter how much effort you put into your work, you're still not satisfied with it until you do *one more thing* to ensure your work is flawless. You keep working and working without stopping to think when enough is enough. Hence, you may hand in your work late or spend so much time plugging away that you put off doing other assignments or engaging in fun activities that I hope are part of your college experience. You may also avoid participating in activities because you know you wouldn't do a perfect job, so why even try.

What are some of the telltale signs of a perfectionist procrastinator? Here's a mini-version of the quiz you took earlier. Do any of these questions resonate with you?

- Do I have a black or white mentality, paying scant attention to the gray area in between?
- Do I berate myself for falling short when my own high standards haven't been met?
- Have others told me I'm being too harsh on myself? Ease up!

The way perfectionists tackle tasks is neither ideal nor sensible. This is no way to live. It's time to create a future for yourself that doesn't wear you out or drive you nuts. Let's begin by looking at three different styles of perfectionism.

Three Perfectionist Styles

Now it's time for me to introduce you to three perfectionists whose mind-sets are crushing their confidence.

Classic Perfectionist

Jennifer portrays the classic image of a perfectionist - a hard worker with cloud-piercing standards. In childhood, she was told to work harder and longer than others so that she would be the best! Do it right or don't do it at all was the motto she heard at home. Jen feels compelled to study more and work harder than her peers. Her problem is compounded by her desire to "get it right" all the time. Thus, despite always working, she feels frustrated that she never has enough time to achieve her lofty goals.

Jen's aware that she imposes too many demands on herself but she just can't seem to settle for anything she sees as *"less than."* Above all, she fears being criticized for not being *"good enough."* Although convinced that she'll never measure up to her older brother Steve (who achieved exceptional grades with little effort), she's determined not to give anyone any reason to fault her performance. It's a paradox - she wants to do her best, yet her work habits practically guarantee that she won't.

Obsessive Perfectionist

Teresa, now working on her doctoral dissertation, believes that she has no control over her perfectionism fearing - with good cause - that it might prevent her from obtaining her degree. Teresa begins most projects in a timely manner. Her strong determination and good work habits seem to guarantee success. Then something happens that throws her off balance. It might be a critical remark from a professor, a sudden dawning of a new procedure or a comment that undermines her self-esteem. Losing confidence in her abilities, she grows increasingly obsessed with every detail until finally her anxiety overtakes her resolve and she stops working on her project, feeling enormous relief. Soon enough, however, she suffers even more stress for giving up on herself. The end result: diminished self-esteem, increased pressure to *"get it right"* and paradoxically, an even stronger urge to put it off till later.

Presently Teresa is stalled halfway through her dissertation. She started by doing an enormous amount of preliminary groundwork, far more than was necessary. When the time came to commit to a final draft, she realized she'd need to eliminate some studies. Stymied over what to do, she became obsessive – unable to decide what to leave in, what to take out. Teresa's now taking a highly refreshing break from her Ph.D. work. Meanwhile, her

academic future hangs in the balance. With additional responsibilities competing for her attention, including a new relationship and a demanding part-
time job, it won't be easy for her to resume working on her dissertation to
see it through to a successful conclusion.

Covert Perfectionist

Keith doesn't appear to be a perfectionist. He's not a hard worker, not a
stickler for detail, nor does he seem to have particularly high standards. He
projects a casual, even flippant attitude about assignments, waiting until the
last minute to do what needs to be done. His rushed work usually pulls him
through in the end, but not with the grades he'd like. He never expresses
much concern about this. Hence, his friends who know he's bright are left
to assume that he's a passive guy with big talents but small ambitions. Nothing, however, could be further from the truth.

Underneath his facade, Keith harbors huge ambitions that intimidate
him. To create an excuse for falling short of perfection, he puts off work
until there's no way he (or anyone else) can expect a first-rate job in the
short time still available. Though Keith doesn't appear to be bothered by his
lackluster accomplishments, inwardly he seethes with frustration blaming
himself for being a poor estimator of time. He's right. However, he has a
more insidious problem. Although he longs to prove his academic superior-
ity, he feels equally pressured to conceal this inner drive. If he were to reveal
it, any failure on his part to excel would be all the more humiliating. How
does he try to resolve this dilemma of wanting to be successful but fearing
he may not measure up? He procrastinates – a far less embarrassing problem
than if he tried hard and still didn't have the goods to measure up.

Different as these students are from each other, they're all struggling
with the ill effects of perfectionism. What they're learning the hard way is
that keeping your nose to the grindstone, burning the midnight oil, and
never taking a break might sabotage your success, not guarantee it.

Four Perfectionist Traits

Either/Or Thinking

Do a perfect job or don't do it at all! Don't seriously consider any middle
ground. This attitude becomes increasingly problematic in higher education
as assignments rarely have perfectly definable outcomes. What's the perfect
research project? The perfect term paper? There's certainly a difference between a poor paper and an excellent one but is there a perfect one? Striving

for a perfect performance only makes sense with simplistic skills - more geared toward elementary school, such as 100% on a spelling test.

Perfectionists often find themselves torn between two alternatives: *giving it all you've got* or *giving it up*. Jennifer usually opts for the former. This sounds good. But seldom does life give her enough time, energy, or motivation to do all that she believes she needs to do to succeed. It's just too much work! Teresa manages to trip herself up by going from non-stop working to exhaustion. Keith sabotages himself by delaying the onset of work, guaranteeing him the perfect excuse for why his work isn't as first-class as it could be.

Impossibly High Goals

Is it possible to have too high a goal? Absolutely! Going for what's unattainable is *not* a great strategy for achieving anything. Pushing yourself beyond your limits is no way to achieve success. High achievers define their objectives with broader, flexible criteria. For example, a marathon runner will judge his performance differently depending on the heat and humidity of the day.

Top athletes set reasonable, season-by-season benchmarks for themselves, designed to help them realize their "personal best." Contrast a high achiever's mindset, *"I'll strive to do my best today,"* with a perfectionist's mindset, *"I must be the best."* Falling short of being the best will trigger deep feelings of inadequacy and guilt for those who demand perfection. With such heavy emotions riding on success, it's no wonder they seek to avoid failure at all costs.

Compulsively doing more than you need to do is one way to try to keep failure at bay. Jennifer squanders precious time and energy keeping her desk and papers meticulously neat. That's one way she deals with her anxiety. For the same reason, Teresa assembles a wider body of data than her thesis requires. Facing the ultimate academic challenge, the attainment of the Ph.D. or MBA, some grad students balk as they never have before. So close to success, yet still not within reach! Rather than gathering up their energy to propel themselves across the finish line, they disperse their energy with self-sabotage. Perfectionists, like Keith, seek to sidestep failure by using procrastination as a defense. Though he presents a casual persona, inside he feels like a fraud. As he gives himself so little time to do assignments, he can't expect to do a perfect job nor can others who listen to his scoffing banter or observe his undisciplined behavior.

Work's an Ordeal – Sigh!

Work quickly becomes an ordeal when you focus on what you're doing wrong, not right; on what you haven't done, not on what you have done.

Being self-critical impedes your ability to relax, as you're always thinking about what else you should be doing. Going for the gold not only keeps you constantly on, it also keeps you striving to maintain an aura of self-sufficiency. As a result, you disregard times you're clearly in need of assistance. Adding to your daily strain is a tendency to brood over past lapses, fret over future obligations.

Jennifer is unable to reflect pleasurably on the past, live comfortably in the present or be optimistic about the future. Keith and Teresa fight *against* time rather than work *with* time.

Fear of Success

It's not only *fear of failure* that creates problems for perfectionists; it's also *fear of success*. Instead of looking forward to success as the joyful end of a long hard journey, you may overwhelm yourself with such life-dampening thoughts as: "Can I live up to the high expectations others will have for me?" - "Will I be able to handle the next challenges I face?" Success raises the bar. You're worried. What if you choke? What if you go down in flames? Though you have the capability to do it, you hold yourself back, not daring to enjoy your triumphant moment.

New challenges, new hurdles, new problems – just thinking about these matters can send perfectionists into a whirlwind. Instead of enjoying their successes, their minds swerve toward all the ways they can now embarrass themselves or even fall flat on their face.

John's Journey
from RIGIDITY to FLEXIBILITY!

When I first met John, his #1 complaint was a growing lack of confidence. He was a junior majoring in economics at one of the nation's highest ranked universities; hence he felt an enormous pressure to succeed. His idealized self-image intensified everything.

I'm a legend in my own mind," John quipped. "I imagine I'll do assignments better than anyone else. Much to my disappointment, it doesn't work out that way." John's deep desire to be the best, coupled with his shaky self-confidence, stirred up a boatload of conflicts. Here's how he described them: "I can't compromise my standards or accept anything less than the best." "I'd rather not do anything at all than do something just mediocre." "Yes, I know I'm my own worst enemy but that doesn't change anything."

The chasm between John's ideal self and real self kept growing. His ideal self, the self he believed he *should* be, was that of a dazzling super achiever.

Yes, he was enrolled in a top university, but everyone in this university was exceptional and he wasn't sure he was measuring up. When he expressed concern to a friend, his friend shot back, "John, cut yourself some slack; you're too hard on yourself!"

Over time, John recognized how his perfectionism and shaky self-confidence were intertwined. An example: "When I receive an A on a paper, I still have doubts. I imagine that the professor must've overlooked my errors. I'm convinced I got away with something. Not a great way to build up my ego, I know."

John's quagmire has a name. It's called *impostor syndrome,* a common phenomenon among perfectionists who believe that no matter how much they achieve, they're never really as competent, qualified or deserving as they appear to be. They're convinced that if someone were to scrutinize them closely enough, their cover would be blown. John couldn't shake the fear that some kind of disastrous calling-to-account would occur at an unpredictable moment. In short: he felt like a phony.

Taunted by his insecurities, John was forever finding reasons to revise his work, making it harder for him to meet deadlines. Referring to an overdue assignment, he griped, "I get to a point where I think I've written a first-rate paper, then I find one more thing that should be included. From then on, it's one delay after another."

Oh, if only John would take **Cardinal Newman's** philosophy to heart:

> *"A man would do nothing, if he waited until he could do it so well that no one at all would find fault with what he has done."*

John doubted that he could alter his patterns. Ironically, while perfectionists seek to control every aspect of what they do, they have trouble believing that control of their success lies *within* them. Instead, they view the *locus of control* as lying somewhere *outside their command* - in the hands of a professor or the fates that be. Hence, no matter how much they do, it's a crap shoot whether it'll work out or not.

When he was younger, John viewed himself as a smart kid who could do practically anything. In high school, he achieved outstanding grades despite his tendency to procrastinate. John's goal at that time was reassuringly straightforward – to graduate with a high GPA and be accepted into a top ranking college. It was hard to lose sight of such a clear goal; hence it was easy for him to stay on track. In college, however, he found it tough to handle not only his academic requirements, which were a lot tougher, but also the more mundane aspects of life like taking care of laundry, shopping, and cleaning up.

John's self-image felt pathetically weak compared to some of his peers who were true geniuses and knew exactly what they were going to do with their lives. Perhaps he wasn't so clever. Perhaps he needed to take a gap year to figure out who he is and what he should do with his life. In those rare quiet moments of solitude, he pictured a life that wasn't so driven, maybe even being a beach bum for a summer. Quite a change for a hard hitting perfectionist!

Though it's tough for most people to shift their style of operating, it's especially taxing for perfectionists for shifting from a familiar pattern to an unfamiliar one inevitably creates uncertainty. *And perfectionists want certainty!* Yet, John had had enough. He's now determined to curb his perfectionism. Here's how he began his change program:

John's First Steps Forward:

John began by *expanding his options* instead of rigidly assuming that there's only one "right" way to do a task. Faced with a new assignment, he'd think about *how* to tackle the task instead of just aiming for perfection. A few examples:

- He'd consider doing an exhaustive search of the research *as well as* doing a more limited search.
- He'd decide whether to finish his term paper *during* spring break or *before* spring break so that spring break might actually be a break.
- He'd think about doing his assignments on his own *as well as* enlisting input from other students and/or teaching assistants.

By pondering alternatives, John trained himself to think *expansively* instead of single-mindedly - some would say *stubbornly*. Over time, he reveled in the freedom and flexibility this new approach offered him. Now onward we march to a potpourri of ideas for you. Excited yet? I hope so!

Your Change Program
from PERFECT to GOOD ENOUGH!

Creating new habits isn't easy but it also isn't as hard as you might imagine. Not if you do it step by step - even baby step by baby step. As you read this chapter, you'll learn many ways to help you overcome your procrastination. However, I *don't* want you to do them all. Try and you'll become overwhelmed!

Hence once you've completed this chapter, return to this section and scroll through the skills I've gifted you. Then, choose no more than *three skills you PROMISE yourself you'll implement NOW*. Practice these skills. Then don't hesitate to compliment yourself when you notice you're feeling less hassled by the need to be perfect.

This change program is designed to be *a reference* for you. So once you've got a few skills under your belt *return for more*. Just don't wait too long!

Now, let's delve into specific strategies to help you curb your procrastination. Know that change often happens slowly and in surprising ways. Be patient with your progress. Ready to begin your journey? Great! I'm psyched. Hope you are too!

THINKING To Get You Moving!

Excellence or Perfection?

Do you think it's better to aim for excellence or perfection? Before you answer, let's examine the difference between the two notions. Dictionaries define perfection as "the condition of being flawless" and "the most desirable state imagined." Excellence is defined as "possessing superior merit" and "remarkably good."

What's your answer? I hope it was excellence, not perfection! Except in something simple, like your grade on a multiple-choice test, perfection is difficult to envision - no less achieve. Contemplate the perfect term paper, the perfect professor, the perfect career. Though you may have a general sense of what would be a magnum opus for you, setting your sights on "perfect" typically fosters disappointment. In contrast, excellence is easier to envision, more realistic to achieve. Striving for excellence *expands* your thinking. Striving for perfection keeps you measuring your work against an abstract standard that may be meaningful only in your own mind.

Many perfectionists were told when they were kids to "always do your best." Sounds like a nice notion, yet it's often impractical. Given the limited time, energy, and resources of our busy lives, you simply *can't* do your absolute best with *everything*. Try to and you'll find yourself low on energy, high on irritability. Hence, instead of having a mind-set that *only* the best will do, conjure up several ways to accomplish a task. Then narrow down the alternatives to the most pragmatic ones - given the time and resources you have available. In making this determination, consider your past experiences handling similar tasks - which strategies worked and which required Herculean effort. Here's a guideline to help you decide how much energy to put into a task:

- If a task isn't important academically, get it done in a run-of-the-mill manner to get it off your plate.
- If a project will account for a large percentage of your grade, put extra effort into it.
- If it's an assignment in a major course that's interesting and important to you, then yes, do your best! Even then, however, strive for excellence rather than outright perfection.

Let's Get Going!

No time like the present to start thinking in a grounded way. Choose an academic assignment you're facing. Think about how you're approaching it or planning to if you haven't yet begun. Now evaluate your approach. Are you making the task bigger than it is? Is there a way to do the task without making it an over-the-top achievement? Rather than aiming to write a seminal paper on each and every assignment, proceed calmly and rationally from the known facts:

- Your professor's stated expectations. Maybe he's only looking for a 1200 word paper while you're planning one twice that length.
- Your genuine interest in the topic. If you're in love with this topic, go ahead and create a seminal paper; if you've little interest in the topic, consider doing an okay job. Yes, okay is often okay!
- Your available time to devote to the project given the deadline date and your other responsibilities. *No, you can't do it all – so choose your priorities!*

Now it's your turn. Open a document. There'll be numerous writing exercises I'll give you, so name this one *Outsmarting Your Perfectionism.* Write down three ways to make one of your academic tasks easier and more enjoyable to do without losing the essential quality of what you want to achieve. Then, listen to the wise part of yourself!

Acknowledge that Perfectionism is Your Problem.

Nobody and I mean nobody is perfect. Not you, nor your favorite athlete, nor that magnificent movie star. Yes, you may have a perfect moment but you won't have a perfect life no matter how hard you try. So, give up being a prisoner of your perfection. Don't insist that every action, deed and event always turn out to be just right. And don't blame others when they're not!

Some perfectionists think that their problems are caused by others. They wonder: "Why should I ease up on my standards? If others did things the way they should be done, there wouldn't be a problem." Let's face it; the world isn't going to change to suit you! Yes, professors could explain things better; they could assign readings more relevant to your life; they could have a better appreciation of your time constraints. They could, they could, they could.

Yet typically, they're not going to. Face it; you have limited control over others. If you repeatedly get fed up with situations - like your professor's remoteness, your roommate's sloppiness, or your friend's lateness, speak up. But don't count on them changing. If they do change, that's a bonus. Be aware that your inability to chill out and accept others as they are may be part of the problem.

> *"Your assumptions are your windows on the world.*
> *Scrub them off every once in a while*
> *or the light won't come in."*
> ~ Isaac Asimov

Manage Your Time By Giving Yourself Extra Time.

Given your high standards, chances are most assignments will take you longer to do than you initially imagine. To make sure you have sufficient time to complete a task, *take your most generous estimate, then add 20%*. For example, if you estimate that you'll need five hours to finish your work, budget six hours. If you're lucky and you don't need the extra hour, you've got it to enjoy any way you want. On the other hand, if you don't initially add the extra hour but wind up needing it, it's inevitable you'll feel stressed.

Similarly, when considering what you want to accomplish in a day, avoid overloading your agenda. Instead, generate a down-to-earth list of possibilities, allowing a 20% margin of time for unanticipated glitches or other opportunities you'd like to take advantage of. Even when you've given yourself extra time, you may find it tough to finish a task. You may hand in a paper late because you believe you need to go over it one more time to make it "perfect." Yes, it may be hard for you to let go of your work if you think you need to edit it once again but you're better off letting go of it than working tirelessly, leaving no time for other assignments or for fun and festivity. Remember that one of your goals is to enjoy the college experience. Am I right? I hope I am!

Be Caring and Compassionate to Yourself.

I bet you're kind to your friends. If so, I have an idea I hope you'll like. Instead of treating yourself harshly, make a conscious, consistent effort to be as compassionate to yourself as you are to your friends. Yes, it makes sense to recognize your errors and realize your shortcomings, but there's no point in overdoing it. Excessive self-criticism is not motivating, it's crippling.

When tackling a tough task, don't intensify your discomfort by disparaging yourself. Disparagement spawns diminished self-esteem which deflates motivation. Hence, think positive thoughts such as, "It'll be tough but I can do it." Or, "Once I get the ball rolling, it'll get easier." If you fail to accomplish your goal, tell yourself "setbacks happen to everyone; it doesn't mean I'm a failure." Experiencing setbacks, making mistakes, even failing entirely to meet your mission are valuable ways of identifying and learning from your limits.

> *"I have learned throughout my life as a composer*
> *chiefly through my mistakes and pursuits of false assumptions,*
> *not by my exposure to founts of wisdom and knowledge."*
> ~ Igor Stravinsky

Stravinsky's classical symphonies written more than a hundred years ago are still revered as musical masterpieces. Now, if Stravinsky learned more from his mistakes than from traditional pursuits of knowledge, so can you!

SPEAKING a New Narrative!

Replace "I Should" with "I Could."

As a perfectionist, you probably keep telling yourself what you *should* be doing. This is draining, as *"should"* denotes the *"right"* way to do something. And who decides what's right? It's an authority – perhaps your professor, your parent, your peer group or your super-ego. Sure, some things you should do; I don't want you thinking that you shouldn't be brushing your teeth or stopping at stop signs. However, as a perfectionist, you've probably adopted an abundance of harsh shoulds that make you believe you have no choice in how or what you do. Rather than raising your productivity, shoulds rouse resistance and resentment, draining your energy and sapping your willpower. So, read on to see how you can soften your shoulds.

Read these two sentences out loud.

- "I *should* study more."
- "I *should* read two chapters every night."

Now replace *should* with *could.*

- "I *could* study more."
- "I *could* read two chapters every night."

What did you notice? Are you aware that *should* implies there's only one *right* way to take care of a responsibility when truly you have the freedom to choose when and how to do your work. Are you aware that *could* is empowering? It carries the mature message that you have the right to make a choice. How much do I need to study? When shall I do the readings? After reflecting on your options, you can then commit to what seems best for you at this time.

Let's Get Going!

Now it's your turn to write a sentence that begins with "*I should.*" Then, change "*should*" to "*could.*" Reread the sentence. What did you notice?

Does the "*could*" sentence offer you more freedom? Does the "*should*" sentence seem more burdensome? If not, try it one more time with another sentence. Again, I'm not suggesting "should" be eliminated from your vocabulary; I'm suggesting you use it judiciously.

Replace "I Must" with "I Choose to."

Must is another word that creates pressure to respond in a manner that may not be of your own choosing. "I must get these problems solved tonight" can either prod you to action or trigger a rebellious reflex which promotes procrastination. Hence, replace *must* with *choose to* and see what happens. "I choose to get these problems solved tonight" reflects more accurately that you yourself are framing the strategy. No need for your rebellious gene to be triggered!

Another possibility: when you say *choose to,* you may recognize that doing the task this evening is *not* your best choice. If you're exhausted, it might be a better idea to get up early tomorrow morning and do it then. Just make sure you're not fooling yourself by making tomorrow the busiest day of the year!

Replace "I Have to" with "I Want to."

There's no need to notice *all* of your word choices but do tune in from time to time. Observe whether you use *have to* frequently, as in: "I have to get an 'A' on this assignment" or "I have to write a 10 page paper this week." *Have to* is one more way of implying coercion. It suggests that you're undertaking an action because you're being *made to.* This makes your work feel more arduous than it needs to be. Instead of *forcing* yourself to act, give yourself an *incentive* to act.

"*I want* to get an 'A' on this assignment" will be easy for you to admit. Saying, "*I want* to write a 10 page paper this week" may seem like pure bull. But that's only if you're reflecting on the short-term, not the long-term. Sure you can think of more enjoyable things to do than write a paper, but let's face it. You're in college not only to enjoy the experience but to get that degree and attain your long-term goals - even if you don't know what they are right now. So, if you can't work up enthusiasm for *wanting to* write the paper, you can certainly acknowledge that you *want to* write it because it's a requirement in a course in which you *want to* get a decent grade.

Lighten Your Self-Criticism.

As a perfectionist, you're inclined to set over-the-top benchmarks for yourself. To temper this tendency, avoid using extreme language when you don't measure up to your own expectations.

Do you hear the difference between these two criticisms?

- *"I screwed up that interview; I'm such an idiot. What's the matter with me?"*
- *"I didn't do as well as I had hoped; I need to upgrade my interview skills."*

Always, always, always be a good friend to yourself. No need for you to be your toughest critic; plenty of others are willing to do that job for you!

Let's Get Going!

Open another new document. Recall a situation when you were disappointed with yourself. Now pretend you are your harshest critic. Yup, I know – you may not have to pretend. Write a paragraph in which you berate yourself for not doing enough, not being smart enough, not being creative enough.

Now imagine that you are your dearest friend. Write a paragraph in which you are kind to yourself, even though you didn't do as well as you had hoped.

Be aware of how you feel when you treat yourself kindly and when you treat yourself harshly. Do you believe you'll do better when you treat yourself well or when you crack the whip without mercy? Why?

ACTION Strategies!

Shorten Your To-Do List.

If you create a daily to-do list, congratulations; it's a good idea. Perfectionists, however, tend to make their list too long. If you put *everything* on your list, you'll practically guarantee being disappointed with what you've done, though you may actually have accomplished a great deal. To prevent this from happening, make your list short and sensible. No need to include *every* little item you'd like to get done. Concentrate, instead, on what's highest priority for you. Resist the impulse to fill up every moment with another to-do task. Make sure you leave unscheduled time so that you can take it easy and enjoy.

If your list is written on paper, use a pen. Then cross off items as you complete them. Don't be like a client of mine who wrote her list in pencil, erasing each item as she completed it. What's wrong with that? No visible record of accomplishment; no recognition of all the work she did; hence, no well-deserved pat on the back. If your to-do list is on a digital device, the same advice applies. Don't delete each item on your list as soon as you've completed it. Instead, put a star next to it to indicate you've done it; a double star for a tough task well done. If you think it's only kindergarten kids who appreciate getting a gold star, you're wrong. We all crave recognition and it doesn't always have to come from other people!

Create a Time Limit for Completing a Task.

Time is finite. We each have 24 hours in a day and a hefty number of those hours are spent sleeping, grooming, eating and doing maintenance activities. Include social activities, fitness workouts, social media and dealing with the unexpected and there's only a limited amount of time left for school work.

To guarantee that you appropriate a reasonable amount of time for your academic work, write out a "time budget" for tasks on your to-do list. I'm sure you know that online activities can inadvertently take up an inordinate amount of time; hence add those to your time budget. And set your phone alarm to go off when time is up. Be sure to check the final chapter of this book to see how the Web can actually nudge you to get back to business. Without such a reminder, it's likely that you'll spend excess time online to the detriment of your other obligations. If your plan isn't working, tweak it don't drop it. And be sure your time budget doesn't have more hours in it than hours in the day!

Do Your Fair Share of Tasks.

At times you'll be participating in a group project. Sometimes it'll be an academic one, like conducting an experiment for a psych class, mounting a theatrical production for a drama class or participating in a study group where each person leads a specific part of the discussion. Other times it will be a non-academic project, like housecleaning with your suitemates.

Since you have a need for things to be done the "right" way, you may be tempted to take on the bulk of the work or to redo what another did. Initially, it may seem like that's no big deal. But even if you can do a task better or faster, it doesn't mean it's a good idea to take over other people's responsibilities. If you do, you'll have less time for your work and you'll end up harboring resentment. Hence, puncture the fantasy that it's no big deal for you to take over a group project, even if your way is indeed better.

Let's Get Going!

Make one deliberate mistake each day. *Whaat??? Are you kidding me?* No, I am not. There's no better way to alter your perfectionistic tendencies than to practice being imperfect. Make a mistake; make it deliberately. Discover what it can teach you. By doing so, you train yourself to cope graciously with blunders and bloopers. What's more, you learn what *truly* needs your precious attention and what you can overlook without any significant consequences.

For example, if you're in the habit of keeping your desk excessively neat, try deliberately leaving it a mess for a whole week. If you make your bed every morning, don't do it for three days in a row. If you're always early for appointments, come ten minutes late to the next one. Sure you'll be uncomfortable doing these things, but so what? Hopefully you'll discover that taking care of some stuff in a below par manner isn't such a big deal. After all, you want some spontaneity in your life, don't you?

> *"Anyone who has never made a mistake*
> *has never tried anything new."*
> ~Albert Einstein

Doing and Being.

A fulfilling life is not only about *doing;* it's also about *being.* Perfectionists typically think they're wasting time if they're not doing something productive. They forget that everyone needs downtime to relax and release the pressure of always being on. Oh, the pressure to perform, the pressure to finish, the pressure to be the best! Allowing the pressure to build and build without release is asking for trouble. So, counteract the tendency to always *do.* Regularly allow yourself time to simply *be.* If you don't know what that means, here are four examples:

- hanging with friends (with no particular agenda)
- taking a casual bike ride or walk
- listening to music
- napping

Now it's your turn. Add four more ideas to this list to help you just *be.* This is important - especially if you're a chronic worker bee. To prevent burnout, you must time off to unwind, let yourself go and relax!

GUIDED IMAGERY
Relax and Let Go!

This exercise is designed to help you recognize and respect your spontaneous side. Whatever image comes to mind is fine. There are no right or wrong answers. Just let your thoughts flow to wherever they want to go.

Choose a comfortable place to sit that's quiet, dimly lit and free from distractions. Take a few deep breaths to relax your body, s-l-o-w-l-y inhaling through your nose, then s-l-o-w-l-y exhaling through your mouth. Let go of any tension or tightness in your body. Allow the thoughts and cares of the day to drift away, leaving your body light, your mind empty.

Read each section of the visualization slowly, pausing for about 20 seconds between each instruction. Or, have someone else read it to you so you can close your eyes, relax and let your mind just be. Let's begin!

Think of a task that's been overwhelming you. Let an *image pop into your mind* that represents this task. See the *image increase in size and strength*. Sense the anxiety you feel when you're swamped with work. Feel the muscular tension in your arms and legs increasing as your anxiety rises.

Now picture the image *slowly shrinking in size*. It's not only getting smaller but attracting all the anxiety and tension you've been experiencing. The smaller the image gets, the more relaxed you feel.

Suddenly, you notice that the *image has morphed into a small black ball which holds all of your worrisome emotions*. See yourself sitting comfortably under a tree in a lovely meadow on a warm, spring day, holding the small ball. Feel the soft grass beneath your body. Feel the warmth of the sun. Feel the gentle breeze in the air. Enjoy seeing the soft, white clouds floating across the sky.

Still sitting comfortably under the tree, *imagine the ball in your hand turning into a helium balloon*. You open your hand, release the balloon and watch it rise up, up, up into the sky until it disappears from view.

Look back at your hand. *See a small red heart lying there*. Press this heart to your chest. Feel it pass into your body easily and magically. Imagine the heart inside you slowly and rhythmically beating, filling you with a sense of peace and well-being.

Hear the nurturing voice of the heart telling you, *"I love you. I accept you. You can relax and still get your work done. It doesn't have to be perfect. You don't have to be perfect. Be kind to yourself - always."* As you embrace the warmth and acceptance of your heart, notice your body relaxing, your mind at ease. Say something nurturing to yourself. Smile and believe it with all your heart.

Take time to absorb the meaning of your visualization. Write down what you want to remember. If you wish, record the instructions so you can play them back at another time to see what new imagery comes to mind.

What's Your Next Step?

Congratulations! You've completed the program for perfectionists. Now take a moment to simply relax and breathe deeply. I hope you don't feel overwhelmed by all the valuable information in this chapter. Yes, you can read it all but you can't absorb it all – at least not right away.

So, return to the change program and choose no more than *three skills you PROMISE yourself you'll implement NOW*. Learning these skills is a prerequisite for outsmarting your procrastination. But it's not just learning them; it's putting them into practice and retaining them. You'll do that, right?

I hope you remember what I said at the beginning of the change program, that it's designed to be *a reference* for you. So, take in what you can use now. Then when you're ready, return to the program to see what's next for you. Just don't wait too long!

And never forget that your personality style has many great qualities. You set high standards for yourself; you're attentive to details; you keep seeking ways to improve what you do. Excellent! Just make sure you know that we all have faults and flaws. And appreciate that good enough is usually good enough, while seeking perfection is often a recipe for misery.

Now might be a good time to take a short break. Get up and stretch. Do a few of your favorite exercises. Grab a snack. If it's mint chocolate chip ice cream, I'm coming over - so save some for me! After your break, move on to the next chapter to continue your journey. There's a lot more to learn.

"It's not the load that breaks you down,
it's the way you carry it."
~ **Lena Horne**

CHAPTER 5

THE DREAMER

...BUT I HATE DOING ALL THOSE DISMAL DETAILS!

Welcome Dreamers! You have many outstanding qualities. You're creative, imaginative, innovative. You may even be a visionary, inspiring others with your captivating ideas. So what could be wrong?

Too often you're the best of thinkers, the worst of doers. You fall in love with an idea, yet skip over doing the details that must be done to bring that idea to fruition. Without dedicated work, your creativity falls flat - leaving you feeling discouraged, possibly demoralized. Fuzzy deadlines, hazy judgments, ambiguous beliefs throw you off course. It's time to zoom in on which ideas are feasible, which are fanciful. If it's feasible, you've got to do the details (even the dismal ones), stay on task (even when you don't feel like it) and take deadlines seriously.

What are some of the telltale signs of a dreamer procrastinator? Here's a mini-version of the quiz you took earlier. See if these questions resonate with you.

- Do I think a lot about what I'd like to accomplish but find it tough to get projects off the ground?
- Do I wait for opportunities to drop into my lap rather than take an active "go get 'em" approach?
- Do I let time drift by with passive activities like watching TV, scrolling through Instagram or just daydreaming?

"The future belongs to those who believe in the beauty of their dreams."

These are the words of **Eleanor Roosevelt**. It's not so beautiful, however, if you're hot to trot but can't get going. Dreamers are famous for indulging in "magical thinking," believing that one day great things will happen for them. How they don't know, when they don't know - yet they believe it will happen. Living in a fantasy world is so seductive! Yet it's no fun when your dreams languish on a back burner, vaporizing into thin air as time marches on.

Without a parent hovering over you, things may get even tougher. Though you may *think* about the work you need to do, actually completing the work is another matter. You may be unclear about the details of the assignment: was it a 1500 or 2500 word paper? You may be casual about a deadline date: was it due this Friday or next Friday? You may be perplexed about why you received a lower-than-expected grade. Perhaps you didn't know what you should have known (e.g. you needed to footnote your references).

Enthusiasm is easy, follow-through is hard. With lots of ideas rolling around in your head, you may find it difficult to settle down to do the work that will make it happen. Even when you start the work, you must keep the momentum going after the initial excitement wanes. "I have many creative ideas," said one of my favorite dreamers, "but somehow my ideas never see the light of day." It took time for this gifted student to appreciate the bottom line: no action; no accomplishments. This is no way for a creative person to live. It's time for you to create a fulfilling future for yourself!

Two Dreamer Styles

Now it's time for me to introduce you to two dreamers whose dispositions are squashing their dreams.

Laid Back Dreamer

Mike illustrates the *"laid back"* variant dreamer who spends too much time dreaming, not enough time doing. Instead of doing the work that might make his dreams come true, he opts for entertaining more riveting notions. Yet, he doesn't hone in on any of these notions long enough for them to serve as viable starting points for serious achievement. When asked about his future, he quips, "I want to be rich and famous and really make a difference but I'm not sure how it'll happen." Then he shrugs his shoulders saying, "I'm buying lottery tickets; maybe it'll happen that way." By his own admission, Mike feels embarrassed that he doesn't know how to make things happen. Such is the legacy of years spent daydreaming rather than performing work in an aware, alert, attentive manner. His pattern is to wait for good fortune to bring him his dreams rather than persevering with actions to make his dreams come true.

When Mike realizes he's got a free weekend to work on his science project, he's initially enthusiastic about it. Yet, he's almost certain to avoid working on the project by binge watching TV or just dozing off. By the time he finally gets around to focusing on his work, it's under heavy deadline pressure. Hence, the end product ends up being a rushed, half-baked job. When he doesn't attain anything remotely like his imagined extravaganza, he's bummed out. To deal with crushing disappointments, Mike relies on elaborate excuse making. *"School's so boring,"* he gripes. *"Creative ideas are so much more interesting."* Mike's girlfriend is aware of his laid-back attitude and has tried to motivate him to action early on. He discounts her concerns, claiming that she's just a worrier by nature. Employing his self-justifying logic, he claims that his procrastination is a bigger problem for her than for him.

Dependent Dreamer

Marcy represents the *"dependent, narcissistic"* type of dreamer. Narcissus is the handsome youth in Greek mythology who spends hours at a time staring rapturously at his own reflection in the water. Marcy has never outgrown the role of being her father's "little princess." Since she still resides at home, it's easy for her to continue living her princess role, neglecting to take significant strides forward in the world outside her magic kingdom. Like a princess, Marcy is self-indulgent. She resists taking timely action on a project because she's "not into it." When she receives a lower than expected grade, she whimpers and pouts like a child begging indulgence from others. She resorts to these same immature tactics to get her parents to do her work for her when she doesn't feel up to it.

Marcy isn't proud of the way she behaves but she feels childishly helpless to act any other way. Her overriding impulse is to dwell in the self-centered, self-satisfying world of her own fantasies. When describing herself to new acquaintances, she's been known to say, "You know that Cyndi Lauper song, girls just want to have fun? That's me!" Addressing her procrastination problem would mean developing a more mature identity. That prospect both intrigues and unnerves her. Who would she be if she changed? She'd find it tough to alter that dreamy image of life that she finds so appealing. The few activities she authentically enjoys doing, like sketching, shopping and socializing take precedence in her life. Other activities, including attending class and serious studying, she sees as *"no fun."* Hence, they become low priority.

Four Dreamer Traits

Gives Insufficient Attention to Details

Dreamers prefer being swept up in generalities rather than tying themselves down to specifics. Hence, they don't give enough attention to the *'who-what-where-when-why-&-how'* details that must be addressed to bring a task to fruition. Though they're typically as smart as any of their peers, consistently ignoring the how-to of a project creates a true lack of competence.

Psychologist **Dr. Martin Seligman** calls this pattern *"learned helplessness."* Once you believe you cannot do a task, (i.e. create a spreadsheet, memorize principles, complete a project) you act as though it's true. In reality, these are skills that dreamers may not want to do, haven't tried to do or haven't given themselves enough time and effort to learn them well. Such tasks will continue to haunt them until they actively approach them instead of passively avoid them.

Once they've convinced themselves that they can't do a task, dreamers rely on others to do their worry and work. Mike, for instance, states that his own procrastination is a bigger problem for his girlfriend than for himself. He doesn't see that his procrastinating compels him to perform a task under such rushed, stressful conditions that he not only fails to learn how to do it well but also develops a dread of ever doing it again. And Marcy resorts to childlike pleading to get others to take on tasks she believes are beyond her.

Passive with Their Responsibilities

Many dreamers invent grandiose fantasies about their future to compensate for their passive performance. Instead of being responsible about earning money, they count on winning the lottery, inheriting money from a surprise source or carelessly racking up debt. Rather than acknowledge their need to put more time and effort into work, they sink back into visions of *someday* and *somehow* they'll astound all with the brilliance of what they've accomplished.

As they indulge in this wait-and-see fantasizing, they put off acquiring the self-discipline and life management skills that would ultimately serve them well in their quest for success. Mike, for example, flips back and forth between spells of disappointment over poorly executed schoolwork and ecstasies of relief with pot-induced reveries. In both states of mind, he neglects to take the necessary steps that could create a well-executed, well-enjoyed lifestyle. Marcy remains passive by living in her timeless fantasy of perpetual fun and childlike innocence, creating a mirage that screens out the requirements of college life. By not being actively engaged in her school work, she unwittingly creates bigger, bleaker problems for her future.

Drifting through Life

Dreamers imagine a reality in which they drift through life without snags or setbacks, effortlessly gliding from A to Z without dealing with the details in between. Their focus on feeling good in the moment induces dreamers to ignore what might make them feel good in the long-term. Instead of taking on tough tasks and thought-provoking challenges, they indulge in insubstantial reveries letting their dreams recede further from reality.

Rather than feeling pride about mastering new proficiencies, Mike resorts to immediate, short-lived pleasures. We can also see this pattern in the way Marcy lives: she's just a girl who wants to have fun, but can't always find it - much less sustain it. Too bad neither Mike nor Marcy appreciates that there are times we must do what we don't want to do or don't know how to do in order to reach our goals.

Overly Dependent on Others

Some dreamers believe that they're ahead of their time. If only others would get their vision, they'd be sitting pretty with fame and fortune. Though others may indeed be impressed with their vision, work still needs to be done. And that is the dreamer's weak spot. How does the dreamer handle the workload? By *persuading parents* to help with (or do) their assignments; by *prevailing upon friends* to take care of their chores; by *convincing teachers* to raise their grades, extend their deadlines or give them second chances.

When dreamers develop a dependency on others to do the grunt work, they simply don't gain the knowledge and skills required to function well on their own. What starts out as a clever maneuver morphs into an unhealthy dependency. This dependency may feel like weakness: "I hate asking others for help." Or, it may be expressed as false entitlement: "I bring the ideas to the table, so why should I have to do the nuts and bolts work?" Not the best strategy for success; not the best strategy for getting along in the world! When dreamers enter the work world with less hands-on, hard-core experience than their peers, they're at a disadvantage from the get-go.

Living so much of their lives inside their heads, it's no wonder that Mike and Marcy haven't developed the needed skills for success. Since they have convinced themselves that they're "special," it's natural for them to believe that others will do for them what they don't wish to do for themselves. Why waste time and energy seeking success the tough way? It would be breaking the faith!

Katie's Journey
from FANCIFUL to FOCUSED!

I still recall the funky denim jacket Katie wore the first time we met. The picture embroidered on the breast pocket was a hot air balloon with colored panels in shades of the rainbow. As I got to know Katie's issues, I realized this balloon was a great metaphor for her dreamer personality: head in the clouds following the wind wherever it took her, brimming with beautiful designs yet vulnerable to collapse in a storm. Yes, images on our personal belongings may reveal aspects of our innermost selves!

Though Katie was in her fifth year of college, she had only accumulated enough credits to be classified as a junior. Every year her pattern had been the same. She'd begin the term with a wave of enthusiasm, throwing herself into her assignments with gusto. Before long, the wave would wither; her incentive to work would waste away; her gusto would go south. Near the end of each term, she'd drop a course or two in order to put all her last minute efforts into passing others. As she described her pattern, Katie accused herself of being spineless. "I don't have a good grasp of time," she admitted with a shrug and a sheepish look. "I spend too much time thinking about an assignment instead of taking action. I try to do better but my energy quickly fizzles out. When I lived at home, my mom would give me a swift kick in the rear to get me going. Now I know it's up to me to get myself going; yet so often I don't."

When I described the six styles of procrastination to Katie, she immediately pegged herself as a dreamer, viewing her problem as a motivational one. *"I need someone to sit me down and make me do things,"* she confessed. Presumably, that's what Katie hoped to find in me - a coach and drill sergeant all bundled into one. However, Katie's issues were more complex than she initially thought. And though having a coach is certainly helpful, I wasn't going to be a drill sergeant. It was not what I wanted to do nor would it be valuable to her in the long run.

It's understandable that Katie believed her salvation lay in others helping her, not in her helping herself. All her life she'd nurtured an image of herself as a "golden girl," ill-suited to deal with the baser metals of life. *"I've always been drawn to people who know how to do things and end up doing things for me,"* she admitted. "I had helicopter parents hovering over me, always available to bail me out - even when I didn't need it. And I have really supportive friends."

When I asked Katie to tell me more about her supportive friends, she replied with a hint of sadness, "Some of them aren't so supportive anymore." Speaking about her boyfriend, she said, "Aaron was supportive but he's become frustrated with me. The other day he called me a class-act excuse maker! Initially, when he saw how far behind I was in my work, he wanted to help. Now when he sees me perpetuating the same pattern, he just shakes his head in disbelief. And there goes any help I might have received."

Like many dreamers, it's hard for Katie to stay with the nuts and bolts of an assignment; it's so much easier to wander off to a more engaging matter. Her friends were more valuable to her now as distractions, not helpers. "I live with three other students in an apartment near campus, so there's always someone to hang with. As I've got zero self-discipline, it's easy to be seduced into doing something more enticing than school stuff."

Katie remembers having vivid fantasizes of stardom when she was a child. "I am an only child. Admittedly, I was doted on." She was told she was prettier and brighter than other kids and her parents thought she could do no wrong. "Whatever I accomplished, Mom and Dad believed was terrific," Katie recalled. "They just wanted me to be happy." Katie's parents meant well but their good intentions didn't beget good results. As their approval was so routinely unconditional, she never developed a genuine sense of validation for accomplishments. Rather than receiving targeted feedback, she received star treatment marinated in starry-eyed dreams.

Katie's early school years were uneventful. After all, she was a smart girl and there were few assignments that required much planning. Her first real challenge was in tenth grade when she was enrolled in an English honors class. "I thought I was in over my head." she told me. "Lucky for me, my best friend was in the class. She'd help me with my assignments. Soon I was imagining that maybe I did belong in honors." This experience is an early example of Katie's dreamer style of working. First she felt overwhelmed by her responsibilities; then she steadily relied on a friend for help which gave her the confidence to continue. Of course, there's nothing wrong with relying on a friend for help - *on occasion*. However, if you never let go of a friend or parent's helping hand, you don't develop the skills you need to be on your own.

Katie is presently trapped in a three-pronged dilemma. She doesn't like structure being imposed on her, she doesn't impose structure on herself and she craves more structure in her life! "Yesterday, I frittered away the whole day. I could have studied or started writing a paper; I did neither. I know now that I need to get a better grip on my time," lamented Katie.

Despite moments of despair, Katie knew she had strengths that could serve her well. She was smart, creative and fun-loving. It therefore pained her to see friends moving ahead when she was falling behind. They'd seek out interesting internships and study-abroad programs while she'd be left dreaming about them. Often, she was consumed with envy. *"Why not me?"* Deep inside, Katie knew the answer to that question. Others went after what they wanted and got it; she didn't! Yet knowing that did not prove to be a sufficient motivator. Indeed, if a friend commented on her lack of effort, she felt hurt. Once, as she was bemoaning to a friend that her instructor gave her a failing grade after excessive absences, her friend offered no sympathy saying, *'what did you expect?'* "I was floored," said Katie. "I came to her for support, not a lecture! Now I know that she was just being honest with me; if I'm not in class, I should expect to suffer the consequences. I admit that at times I'm a bit late to get the rules of the game."

Katie's First Steps Forward:

Katie was so oriented toward "feeling good" that I knew she needed to become more self-disciplined. Hence, I advised her to reframe her thoughts by asking herself, *"Will doing this make me feel good **about myself** or will I just feel good for the moment?"*

Katie was delighted with how effective this simple shift in thinking was. "At first I felt stupid asking the question. Then one day I was driving to the mall, asked myself the question and knew immediately that going to the mall was not going to make me feel good about myself. I turned right around and went back to my room to hit the books. Truth be told, I didn't like it but I was glad I did it!" As we worked together, Katie adopted additional skills to vanquish her inclination toward dreaming at the expense of doing. Time for you to learn them too!

Your Change Program
from DREAMER to DOER!

Creating new habits isn't easy but it also isn't as hard as you might imagine. Not if you do it step by step - even baby step by baby step. As you read this chapter, you'll learn many ways to help you curb your procrastination. However, I *don't* want you to do them all. Try and you'll become overwhelmed!

Hence once you've completed this chapter, return to this section and scroll through the skills I've gifted you. Then choose no more than *three skills you PROMISE yourself you'll implement NOW*. Be patient with your progress. And be sure to say nice things to yourself when you notice you're practicing these skills, not just thinking about them.

This change program is designed to be *a reference* for you. So once you've got a few skills under your belt, *return for more*. Just don't wait too long! Now, let's delve into specific strategies to help you curb your tendency to dream rather than do. Once they become part of your routine, your creativity will pay off – big time. Ready to begin your journey? Great! I'm psyched. Hope you are too!

THINKING To Get You Moving!

Differentiate Goals from Dreams.

Enjoy your dreams! Appreciate, however, that dreams are different from goals. Goals require you to put in time and effort - often a lot of it - in a series of structured steps. So, if you're picturing an "A" on your final, a completed dissertation, a scholarship to a prestigious school, a job contract that will whisk you from graduation to career success, know that to make your dreams come true you must turn them into goals. A goal is composed of a plan with an explicit structure, including:

- *Objectives* that are clearly defined.
- *Steps* you'll take to achieve your objectives.
- *Time frames* you'll meet to complete each step.
- *Resources* you'll use to attain your objectives.
- *A goal line* to know when you've achieved success!

Let's say you'd like to raise your grade in a tough course you're taking. You can *dream* about it, imagining reveries such as: getting an A on your final exam; your professor being impressed with your term paper; getting a high-five from your dad for your achievement. Or you can set a *goal* for yourself, detailing what you'll *do* to achieve your goal. Your stated objective might be, "I want to improve my grade before finals week." Then delineating the precise *action steps* you'll take to achieve your goal, such as: study six extra hours a week, hire a tutor, speak to your professor about how to proceed with your term paper, create definitive time frames to accomplish each step. Notice the difference between dreams and goals? Excellent! Now onward we march.

Use the "5 W's, 1 H" Method.

Your mind may be buzzing with interesting ideas but until you ground your thinking, nothing will happen. Hence, get into the habit of asking relevant questions that begin with: *Who, What, When, Where, Why* and *How.* Here's a model to help you get started, based on your desire to get a summer internship that will advance your career aspirations:

- **Who** do I want to work for? (Individuals or organizations?)
- **What** type of internship will I seek?
- **When** will I begin my search?
- **Where** would I like to work?
- **Why** do I want a summer internship? (Clarify your ideas.)
- **How** might this internship aid my career aspirations? (Be specific!)

This exercise is designed not only to help you turn your dream into a solid step-by-step action plan, although that by itself would be a laudable goal, but also to prompt you to become *motivated* to take action instead of just wishing and hoping.

No More Revelling in Being "Special."

Resist the temptation to engage in self-stroking reveries of being smarter, more talented or more creative than others. Such fantasizing can mean you avoid taking the necessary action to cultivate your talents. There are countless ways you can create self-deluding gaps between your private image of yourself and your public image. Hence, it's a good idea to stay on top of your thoughts by asking yourself questions like, "Am I inflating this story?" or "Am I getting carried away here?"

For instance, you may present yourself in a more favorable manner by saying you failed an exam because you refused to take it seriously on principle, leaving the reluctant teacher with no choice but to give you a failing grade. Or, you may be thinking one thing but say something entirely different to create a good impression, such as telling your friends that you're not worried at all about an upcoming exam when deep inside you're dreading it. Such discrepancies between your "real self" and your "dream self" undermine your belief in yourself. The upshot: it becomes easier for you to sink into an avoidance pattern, increasing your tendency to procrastinate.

Let's Get Going!

Challenge yourself to pay more attention to details. Have you had the experience of learning a new word, then suddenly you seem to see that word everywhere? Obviously, the word has been there all the time; you just never focused on it. Since dreamers tend to gloss over the details, it's time to reverse that direction.

Let's do an exercise: Look around you right now. Without getting up from your seat, notice something you hadn't noticed before. Observe either a new object or a new detail about a familiar object. Be curious about what you've observed.

Now notice something new about your own body. Put your left hand out in front of you. Pretend you're a neurosurgeon specializing in hands.

What details do you observe that you hadn't noticed before? Now pretend you're an artist who's going to paint a picture of your hand? What details do you notice?

Now put both hands out in front of you. Notice three differences between your two hands. Yes, there's always more to observe. As a dreamer, your creativity is your strength; your lack of attention to details is your weakness. Once you begin to notice the details that make up the whole, there'll be no stopping you!

SPEAKING A New Narrative!

When You Say "I'll try to," try to!

"I'll try to" is fine to say, if you're sincerely going to make an effort to do the task. However, if you just keep saying you'll *try to* but don't back it up with action, your words will be blowing in the wind. I can tell you with 100% certainty that if someone asks you to lift up a couch, you can legitimately say *"I'll try to."* If you're asked to lift up a pillow, *"I'll try to"* makes no sense. You either do it or you don't. Get the difference?

So, be cognizant of how often you say "I'll try to." Say it only when you *know* you're going to take action. Otherwise, it's just a way to continue dreaming – without doing. Yes, some things are hard to do and success is not guaranteed, like *"I'll try to* raise my GPA this semester." But other things are definitely doable, like *"I'll try to* work on my report this evening." So limit your *"trying to!"* If it's a task that's definitely doable, make a defined timeline for getting it done, such as "I'm sitting my butt down *right now* to get this report done!"

Let's Get Going!

By now you know this is not just a book to read. It's filled with actions for you to take. So, let's get going! I wouldn't be surprised if you make a lot of statements that begin with *"I'll try to"* or *"I wish."* So, say one out loud now. C'mon, out loud! Then change your first words to *"I am"* or *"I will"* and insert a time as to *when* you'll do it. Then say the sentence again. Now, keep your word! You don't want to disappoint yourself again, do you?

Change Vague Language to Focused Language.

Vague language is a bit like molding clay. You can shape it anyway you want, making it into a realistic work of art or mashing it into something that has no shape or form. It's a bit like saying *"someday, I'll do it,"* which could be soon or never. Or, *"when I get a chance,"* which may mean in an hour, next month or umm, who knows when? Or, *"as soon as I can,"* yeah, don't hold your breath! As you can see, vague language gives you a blanket excuse to let matters drift. Hence, instead of drifting, specify *when* you'll do a task. Change:

- "Someday, I'll organize my desk (sigh!)" to
  "Today I'm organizing my desk!"
- "When I get a chance, I'll call home" to
  "Tonight at 8, I'll call home."
- "As soon as I can, I'll finish my paper" to
  "This evening, I'll finish my paper."

Continue to be fuzzy with your timing and you'll frequently find yourself on the defensive - explaining to others why you didn't do what you said you'd do. Vague language not only confounds others, it may also confound you! You may say:

- "I have a cash-flow problem" when you're really heavily *in debt.*
- "It's a lazy day today" when it's *you* who feels lazy.
- "I'm getting out of shape" when truly you *are* out of shape.

It's helpful to know what your reality is - clearly and candidly - so that you're not fooling yourself or others. Initially you may feel awkward altering your speech patterns. But stay with it! It'll become more natural with practice and your perk will be a firmer grip on "what is." And who knows, that molding clay may remodel itself into a splendid work of art!

Good-bye, Grandiose Talk.

No need to use grandiose language to bolster your self-esteem.

- "I deserve a better grade."
- "I'm the smartest person in my class."
- "I should have more time to finish my lab work."
- "I shouldn't have to attend class if I can pass the final."

These types of statements reflect more wishful thinking than reality. Though there may be a grain of truth in them, that grain is too tiny to accurately represent reality. When you catch yourself on the verge of making a self-inflating statement, see if you can back it up with facts. When you do, your statement will be rendered less extreme.

For example, rather than saying, "I deserve a better grade," clarify why you think that's true by saying, "I deserve a better mark on the second essay question because I covered each of the points discussed in class." Once you base your belief on facts, you can open up a dialogue with your professor. If she agrees, great! You've made a point and proved it. If she disagrees and explains why the lower grade still stands, hopefully you'll gain an appreciation of her viewpoint. It's possible your essay did indeed cover the points, but not in depth.

ACTION Strategies!

Write Down Dates.

It's helpful to provide yourself with *a visual tool* for measuring your progress by writing down milestones and deadlines. An example:

- **Open a new document.**
  Write your *goal* and the *completion date*. Be specific. "Psych Class" is not nearly as helpful as "Paper for Psych Class on The Paranoid Personality: Completion date May 1st."
- **Create a timeline for the project.**
  At the top write today's date; at the bottom write the completion date. Between the two dates, list the major tasks you'll need to do to achieve your goal. The tasks might be:
  - ✓ Research the paranoid personality
  - ✓ Decide on 3 reference books
  - ✓ Create an outline
  - ✓ Write your first draft
  - ✓ Edit the draft
  - ✓ Add additional references
  - ✓ Re-read your paper
  - ✓ Edit once more
  - ✓ Complete and celebrate!

If a task seems overwhelming, break it down into smaller tasks. As you complete each smaller task, you'll feel a *surge of success* instead of a fear of failure. As you continue to progress, reward yourself with a fist pump and a compliment. This step-by-step progress may not be as exciting as dreaming about grandiose accomplishments, but it will pay off!

Let's Get Going!

Surely, you don't want to keep living in the land of unfulfilled dreams. So now is the time to create your own written plan for achieving a goal. Think of a complex chore (personal or academic) that you want to or need to complete. Write down the *specific steps* you'll need to do to turn your goal into a reality. Create *a timeline* for each of the milestones. Now, get going! You want to be successful in life, don't you?

Oops, that reminds me. I need to find a first-rate book cover designer. I shall do that tomorrow. No, really I shall. One thing you should know about me - I take my own advice. Of course, by the time you're reading this, you've seen the cover. Hope you like it!

Finish your Projects.

Dreamers have a reputation for allowing time, energy and goals to drift away as they watch TV, check their phones, nap or hang with friends. If you're passive on occasion - no problem! If you stay in that state too often - a big problem! It won't always be your first choice to push yourself to study harder or to forge ahead on an intricate paper. However, in the long run the self-confidence and self-respect you'll gain from *completing* these activities will be worth it. Once you develop a habit of finishing what you set out to do, don't be surprised if you keep racking up success after success!

Use a Calendar.

Like many of today's organizational tools, a calendar can be on your phone, laptop or it can be an old-fashioned paper calendar. It matters not what form it takes. It matters a lot whether you utilize it properly – recording your appointments and checking the calendar often to see what's there. Any system works if you work the system. The converse is also true. *No system works if you don't work the system.* So make sure whatever system you choose, high tech or low tech, you make it work for you.

Imagine that your calendar is your personal professional organizer that exists to remind you of your responsibilities. Make sure you incorporate into it: classes, labs, study times, computer time, library time, planned events, social commitments, and anything else you want to remember. I repeat, *check your calendar frequently.* It does you no good if you write it down, then promptly forget about it. Check off each responsibility when you've completed it or move it over to the next day if there's still work to be done. Check out future entries well in advance, so you're not taken by surprise by what's coming up. A well maintained calendar helps you structure your time so that you can be on top of what you need to do.

In addition to my phone, I like to use a large calendar book, 8.5 x 11 inches. This makes it highly visible, thus hard to misplace. I have plenty of space each day to record items in specific time slots. I record what I need to do as soon as I commit to it, whether that's an appointment with a client, a social activity, a call I need to make or a paper to complete. If an activity requires transportation time, I make sure that's accounted for too. This is what works for me. Now, you figure out what will work for you!

Let Go of Fantasy Lineups.

Whereas perfectionists tend to create lists that are overly detailed, dreamers often don't create lists at all or create ones that are more fantasy lineups than reality. What's a fantasy lineup?

- Become a millionaire before age 30
- Own my own computer business straight out of college
- Become an award-winning actor

This is not to say that these goals are necessarily out of reach for you. If that's what you want, more power to you! However, they're not going to happen magically. You need a grounded to-do list that delineates the steps you'll take to get you from A to Z. You must deal with the details (even those yucky ones) to attain your ambitions. Using the calendar you created in the above exercise will train you to distinguish between tasks you've committed to accomplishing *on a particular day* and those you think you'll get to *sometime down the road.* As a dreamer, you may be inclined to let day-to-day responsibilities drift into the future-to-do category, even when it gets you in hot water!

Be Proactive with Your Future.

Though you're probably not ready to launch your career, there are still actions you can take *now* to help you create a dream future. You might visit the career office to discuss job opportunities, research companies in your field, look for a summer job *before* summer arrives.

If you want to be on top of your game, you've got to be proactive, not wait for opportunities to drop into your lap. That way you become *an active participant* in your own future. Hence, start scheduling one *looking ahead task* every other week. Then take a deep breath, smile and pat yourself on the back as you see that some dreams actually do come true!

> *"I find that the harder I work the more luck I seem to have."*
> ~ Thomas Jefferson

Move!

It's important that you don't get seduced into doing an abundance of passive activities. Rather than lounging in bed, playing video games or hanging out, get involved in activities that generate more energy - like exercise or participating in a sport. Find an activity you like to do. For me, it's tennis and yoga. What is it for you? If you have trouble getting motivated to move, use an alarm to spur you into action. If you're napping but told yourself you'll get to the gym by 2 P.M., set your phone to beep 30 minutes before. Throw cold water on your face, do a few stretches and get going - whether you feel like it or not!

When you become active, you'll be enacting the second part of Isaac Newton's first law of motion: *"An object at rest tends to stay at rest and an object in motion tends to stay in motion."* Next time you're simply sitting and staring into space, remind yourself that you're an object at rest. Until you shift into motion, you'll stay at rest. So, discover the motion that makes you come alive. Then get going. Can you tell I'm a big believer in taking action? And not grumbling about it but enjoying it!

Be Social.

If you're inclined to stay by yourself in your own little dream world, make a concerted effort to be more involved with others. Here are ways to do this:

- *Create* or join a study group.
- *Invite* a classmate to lunch.
- *Ask* classmates how they're handling a course requirement.
- *Set up i*nformational interviews to learn about prospective careers.
- *Speak* with fellow students about their perspectives on professors. It's great to learn which professors are tedious and tiresome and which are inspiring and invigorating *before* you sign up for a course.

GUIDED IMAGERY
Relax and Let Go!

It may seem counterproductive for you to do guided imagery as it's likely you already spend too much time in your head. However, this exercise is specifically designed to help you turn those abstract dreams into attainable achievements.

Choose a comfortable place to sit that's quiet, dimly lit and free from distractions. Take a few deep breaths to relax your body, s-l-o-w-l-y inhaling through your nose, then s-l-o-w-l-y exhaling through your mouth. Let go of any tension or tightness in your body. Allow the thoughts and cares of the day to drift away, leaving your body light, your mind empty.

Read each section of the visualization slowly, pausing for about 20 seconds between each instruction. Or, have someone else read it to you so you can close your eyes, relax and let your mind just be. Let's begin!

Picture yourself standing in a park *holding the strings to 3 helium balloons,* one red, one yellow, one green. You look up and admire the balloons swaying in the sunny sky. As you look closely, you notice *a dark shape inside each one* – though you can't make out what the shapes are.

Imagine the balloons bumping into one another, tugging on the strings you're holding. The motions are increasing in intensity until it becomes uncomfortable to keep holding them. You look around and *notice a waist-high pole in the ground with a hook* on the end of it. You *tie all three balloons to* the hook.

Curious about what's inside the balloons, you grab hold of the string to the *red* balloon, pull it down to the ground and burst it open with a pin. There, among the balloon fragments, is *a flat long wooden piece you recognize as the floor to a miniature house.* Place it on the ground in front of you.

Next you grab hold of the string to the *yellow* balloon, pull it down to the ground and burst it with a pin. There among the fragments are *four smaller wooden pieces that you recognize as the walls to the house.* You fit each wall into a groove on the floor piece, noticing doors on each wall that can swing open.

Finally you grab hold of the string to the *green* balloon, pull it down to the ground and burst it with a pin. There among the fragments are *several pieces of furniture including a cozy chair, a warm rug and creative works of art.* You choose what you like, adding them to the house. Finally you notice *a small tile roof* that you place on top of the four walls of the house.

You step back and admire *the miniature house you've just built.* Suddenly, you see it growing in size until it becomes *an attractive full-sized house.* You enter the house, noticing the cozy chair you placed inside, the rug you chose and a lovely piece of art. You sink into the chair, relax and hear a voice saying, *"When you work diligently and finish what you set out to do, your creativity will flourish."*

Continue to relax, noticing how good you feel when you finish what you set out to do. Keeping your body relaxed, reflect on three tasks you can do in real life that will help make your dreams come true. Write down what you're thinking. Then, get moving! If you wish, record the guided imagery so you can play it back at a later date to see what new imagery comes to mind.

What's Your Next Step?

Congratulations! You've completed the program for dreamers. Now take a moment to simply relax and breathe deeply. I hope you don't feel overwhelmed by all the valuable information in this chapter. Sure, you can read it all but you can't absorb it all - at least not right away.

So, return to the change program and choose no more than *three skills you PROMISE yourself you'll implement NOW!* Learning these skills is a prerequisite for outsmarting your procrastination. But it's not just learning them; it's putting them into practice and retaining them. You'll do that, right?

I hope you remember what I said at the beginning of the change program, that it's designed to be a *reference* for you. So take in what you can use now. Then when you're ready, return to the program to see what's next for you. Just don't wait too long!

Never forget that your personality style has many great qualities. You're creative, you're imaginative, you have interesting ideas. Excellent! Now use those traits to advance your education. This will require you to stay with problems longer and *do* those dismal details, whether you want to or not.

Now is a good time to take a short break. Get up and stretch. Do some lunge walks. Grab a snack. If it's sea salt caramel ice cream, I'll join you! Then move on to the next chapter to continue your journey. There's a lot more to learn.

> *"It's not that I'm so smart,*
> *it's just that I stay with problems longer."*
> ~ **Albert Einstein**

CHAPTER 6

THE WORRIER
...BUT WHAT IF I MAKE THE WRONG CHOICE?

Welcome Worriers! You have many admirable qualities. You're caring and conscientious; you're concerned about your future. You're mindful of safety issues. You're aware of details others gloss over. So what's holding you back?

Let's face it; it's tough for you to take challenges in stride. Stewing over what might go wrong and worrying about what might happen if.... makes it impossible to relax. Keep playing it safe and you'll never know how high you can fly. In this chapter, you'll gain a better understanding of your worrier personality and how it handicaps you from being all you can be.

What are some of the telltale signs of a worrier procrastinator? Here's a mini-version of the quiz you took earlier. See if these questions resonate with you.

- Do I hesitate to leave my comfort zone, avoiding whatever might make me feel anxious?
- Do I paralyze myself before working on a project by worrying about the "what ifs"?
- Do I have difficulty making decisions, frequently vacillating about what I should do?

"Procrastination is like a credit card.
It's a lot of fun until you get the bill."
Christopher Parker

Though procrastination may be fun for some, if you're the worrier type it's sheer distress from the scary start till the panicky end. Dreading what might happen takes a toll on your ability to focus, make decisions and do what needs to be done. Even after you make a decision, you still worry about whether it was the right one. Though many students are anxious about their future, worriers are distinguished by the frequency, depth and severity of their angst.

Rather than taking challenges in stride, you experience them as potential catastrophes. Rather than honing in on what might go right, you obsess over what might go wrong. This angst is emotionally and physically draining. And what makes it particularly troublesome is that despite all your worrying, nothing productive is achieved. This is no way for you to deal with challenges in college or in life. You deserve better. It's time for you to create a future for yourself that's less anxious, more fun. I hope you want that too!

Two Worrier Styles

Now it's time for me to introduce you to two worriers whose anxiety keeps crushing their confidence.

Frozen by Fear Worrier

Heather describes herself as a "bundle of nerves," freely admitting that she doesn't work well under pressure. "I panic easily. It's not like I'm running around screaming like a crazy person. It's that my high level of stress incapacitates me. When I'm nervous, I can't focus, I can't think well, I can't make a decision. I'm paralyzed by worry, exhausted even though I haven't done anything to tire me out!"

Heather agonizes over her responsibilities. Too nervous to tackle a tough task, she puts it off until there's a better time, only that time never arrives. Too nervous to contact a TA to clarify an assignment, she delays doing it until it's too late. Rather than trusting her intuition, she has a nagging need to ask for help with her independent research. Yet she hesitates to ask as she doesn't want to appear foolish. Then, when her work falls short of her expectations, she berates herself for being so stupid. Heather, frozen in fear, is afraid to move out of her comfort zone to get the comfort she craves.

Overly Needy Worrier

Scott hastily turns to friends for direction, for he lacks faith in himself. He has difficulty making his own decisions and following through on them once they're made. "I need to choose a major," he said, "yet I can't commit. I keep thinking that if I make a bad choice it'll ruin my life." It's not only major decisions Scott frets over; it's minor ones as well. A few examples:

- Unsure how to handle an assignment, he gnaws over options until deadline time closes in. Then he impulsively chooses any option just to get it over with.
- Thinking it might be a good idea to throw a party for his brother's birthday, he dithers endlessly over how to organize it and who to invite until his mom takes over the planning for him.
- For weeks prior to registration, he can't decide what courses to take. Then he lets his friend decide for him as they chat about options.

Scott is consistently attracted to the deceptive security of doing nothing at all until time is up. Though he loathes uncertainty, he unwittingly cultivates it. Unable to trust his own judgment, he relies on others to make decisions for him, even for what his major will be! Both Heather and Scott are caring, conscientious students. Yet their worrying is wrecking their college experience as they seek safety in their too-tight-comfort-zone.

Why do they seek to stay with the familiar? Because they don't want to become so distressed that they panic. Most people who have never experienced a panic attack think of it as being out-of-control, screaming hysterically. But rarely is panic expressed that way. It's usually a flight response (*I have to get out of here!*) a fight response (*I can't stand him!*) or a freezing response (*stay immobile and inactive*).

Four Worrier Traits

Difficulty Dealing with Change

Like Dorothy in The Wizard of Oz, worriers can be enthralled by new people and new experiences – in their dreams. In waking life, however, their instinct is to head for home. What's unfamiliar triggers discomfort; discomfort triggers fear; fear is to be avoided. Even small tasks can loom as dormant difficulties. Cleaning out their mess of papers can become "overwhelming," hence too tough to do. Why? Because confronting the mess means making ill-at-ease decisions: what to discard; what to file; where to put things.

Worriers may yearn for the excitement of new activities, new places to visit and new people to meet. However, when confronted with taking the leap into the unknown, they tend to stay put choosing safety over adventure. If that means being bored, blue or bummed out, so be it; anything's preferable to going out on a limb. Their cautionary mindset is reinforced with a host of "what ifs?" *What if* I fail? *What if* I make a fool of myself? *What if* I make the wrong choice? The list is never ending.

Spinning a too-tight cocoon deprives worriers of the opportunity to break out, spread their wings and fly. We see this in the way Heather holes up in her room, allowing her worries to overwhelm her, while Scott lets others make decisions for him instead of taking a risk and making the decision for himself.

Fearful of Doing Something Wrong

Worriers are afraid of doing something *wrong,* which isn't limited to actions that are morally or ethically bad. Their definition of *wrong* covers a vast territory. It can be anything that's unorthodox, uncomfortable, unsuitable or just plain risky. Hence, they may shun an undertaking because they're not sure how to handle it. Or, they may commit to doing it but postpone working on it for as long as possible.

Heather, for example, turns a difficult task into a repellent nightmare by focusing on anything and everything that might go wrong. Scott puts off writing his term paper because he's consumed with concern about how to handle it.

Tentative Decision-Making

When worriers make a decision, they're still inclined to change their minds for they're never quite sure if it's the right one. If worriers are compelled to commit they can, but not with the confidence and enthusiasm that ensures success.

Heather knows she needs to study. Yet, her worrying interferes with her ability to absorb information, leaving her with the belief that studying won't pay off. This then becomes a self-fulfilling prophecy. It's no wonder she thinks that nothing ever works out for her! Scott shows the same brand of half-hearted, doomed from the start commitment when he's registering for classes. Instead of enthusiastically choosing his courses, he passively allows his friend to decide for him. Later on, he can justify backing away from them. After all, he wasn't the one who chose them in the first place!

Needing Lots of Reassurance

Lack of confidence compels worriers to turn to more confident people for reassurance and direction. In this respect, they're like scared kids, looking for someone to show them the way. Clearly one's friends, teachers, and advisors can be excellent resources, but it's not their job to function as parents or therapists. When worriers rely heavily on others, they jeopardize their own growth as well as the integrity of those relationships.

Heather's dependency on others is obvious when she hopes that they'll anticipate and meet her needs. This *dependency tendency* is even more apparent in the way Scott can't make a decision about how to organize his brother's birthday party, eventually letting his mom take over.

Melissa's Journey
from UNEASY to AT EASE!

When I first met Melissa, her anxiety was blatant. She had difficulty looking me in the eyes, had a perplexed look on her face and was nervous about how I might judge her. "I need you to tell me what's wrong with me," she declared. "I promise myself I'll be on top of assignments yet I always fall behind. It's not like I'm having fun or anything; I just get so frantic over the work that I can't get moving. It's tough for me to focus, so I just sit there letting time waste away." Like many others, Melissa felt powerless over her tendency to procrastinate.

By the time we met, Melissa's troubles had seeped into several areas of her life. When worried, she'd shovel in junk food. The 20 pounds she gained since last year made her feel terrible but she felt powerless to change her habits. She was also having trouble sleeping, unable to let go of the worries of the day. Melissa described her apprehension this way: "I'm frequently freaking out. I can't go with the flow like my friends tell me to. I feel stupid; I envision the worst. I tell myself I should work on a paper early because I can't stand working under pressure. Then I go ahead and procrastinate anyway. It doesn't make sense; I hate pressure, yet I keep putting pressure on myself!"

Not only was Melissa impairing her health, she was also impairing her career goals. An example: one of her professors took a liking to Melissa and told her about a part-time job at a nearby law firm. The woman offering the job was the professor's friend, hence Melissa had a good chance of getting hired if she interviewed well. "When I left the professor's office I was ecstatic," she sighed, "but then I got so nervous about phoning the firm that I found every reason in the book why this wasn't the right time to call. I told myself I had to do research on the firm, revise my resume and practice my interview skills. By the time I called, it was too late. Now I wonder if I sabotaged my chances as a way of protecting myself from being rejected. And what do I have to show for all my worrying? Just one more disappointment to add to my list!"

Melissa recalled that though she had good grades in high school, she had always shied away from taking risks. "My goal was to be praised by my teachers," she confessed. "I knew I was bright but never thought of myself as creative. My art projects were pretty but not special. My reports were nice but not exceptional. 'Play it safe' was my mantra. But everything I did was so ordinary, it made me feel ordinary. I missed out on things I might have enjoyed if only I could have let myself take a risk."I pointed out to Melissa how often her actions were chosen with the express purpose of maintaining familiar ways. Even when her ways were unfulfilling, they were predictable, hence safe.

Melissa's first years in college were an eye opener for her. "Living on my own a thousand miles away from home was tough," she admitted. "I'm the youngest in a large family. I always had someone to turn to when I was growing up, particularly my mom. My first year in college, I was on the phone with her all the time asking for assistance. The next year I called less often only because I felt embarrassed about it - none of my friends were doing it."

As we worked together, it became clear that Melissa often experienced *"anticipatory anxiety."* This is when you experience more anxiety *before* an event than when the event actually occurs. Such anxiety is fortified by a never ending cycle of "what if" questions, such as: *What if* my research project isn't what the professor wants? *What if* the lab work is too technical for me? *What if* I take a point of view that's wrong?

Melissa's worrying also had an adverse effect on her personal relationships. Here's a particularly poignant example: "There are times I wait so long to make a decision that the decision is made for me. Last year, I met Adam. He was a great guy; strong, secure, good-looking. Wow, what a combination of traits I thought; he's perfect for me! But instead of making me feel more secure, he began controlling me. I had no identity, no voice. I knew I needed to end the relationship but I didn't know how to do it. I kept putting off telling him how I felt. I put it off so long, I never had a chance. One day, he dumped me, saying I was no fun anymore."

One more problematic plight for Melissa: "I should've completed my grad school applications months ago but I kept stalling. Then I thought maybe my friends could help me out but I saw how busy they were with their own stuff so I didn't ask them. Anyway, I had doubts that I'd get into the schools I picked so I thought, why bother?" Melissa's defeatist opinion was based on fear, not fact. She wasn't applying to highly competitive schools and she had good grades despite all her worrying. Yet, once again, she repeated the pattern of:

- Harboring a pessimistic attitude about her capabilities.
- Postponing work on whatever seemed difficult.
- Seeking help from a position of weakness (*"I can't do it"*) instead of strength (*"let's collaborate"*).
- Feeling fearful about her future, peeved with her past.

Melissa's First Steps Forward:

Melissa started with a small change that made a large, lasting impact. She consciously and deliberately approached challenges with two distinct steps:

- First decide whether you're going to commit to an action. No more *"maybe"* - a definite *"yes"* or *"no."*
- Second if it's *"yes,"* no more backtracking. Instead, focus on the steps you'll take to make your goal a reality!

Melissa found this approach to be extremely helpful. "Yes," she decided, swallowing her mounting fears. "I do want to go to grad school. I promise myself I'll complete my applications in two months. The first draft I'll do on my own; then show it to my mom to get her input. Then I'll hire a consultant to fine-tune my application." To keep herself calm and composed, she took a few deep breaths, slowly rolled her shoulders and compiled a list of short, simple and to-the-point affirmations. Her favorites were: *"Yes, I can! - Trust yourself! - Stay calm!"*

As you know, I love great quotes. Some people can say in a few words just what you need to hear. Hence, I introduced Melissa to author **Erica Jong.**

> *"I have accepted fear as a part of life and I've gone ahead despite the pounding in my heart that says turn back, turn back, you'll die if you venture too far."*

Though Melissa had never read any of Jong's books, she related right away to her philosophy, recognizing how frequently her actions had been controlled by fear. As we continued to work together, Melissa smiled more, frowned less as she learned skills to help her overcome her debilitating anxiety.

Your Change Program
from TENSE to TRANQUIL!

Creating new habits isn't easy but it also isn't as hard as you might imagine. Not if you do it step by step - even baby step by baby step. As you read this chapter, you'll learn many ways to help you curb your procrastination. However, I *don't* want you to do them all. Try and you'll become overwhelmed.

Hence, once you've completed this chapter, return to this section and start scrolling through the skills I've gifted you. Then, choose no more than *three skills that you PROMISE yourself you'll implement NOW*. Take on too much and it's likely you'll panic. So be content with what you can handle without a lot of worrying.

I've designed this change program to be *a reference* for you. Thus, once you've got a few skills under your belt, *return for more*. Just don't wait too long! Be patient with your progress. And say nice things to yourself when you notice you're feeling more confident. Ready to begin your journey? Great! I'm psyched. Hope you are too!

THINKING To Get You Moving!

Know that Avoiding Making a Decision is a Decision.

Picture yourself standing at a fork in the road. You can choose the left fork…the right fork…or you can continue standing at the crossroads forever. Hopefully, this imagery will help you appreciate that *not* making a decision is a decision—the decision to stay right where you are.

If you avoid making a decision for long periods of time - or forever - you place yourself at the mercy of others or at the mercy of fate. Is this your aim? Do you really want *others* to make decisions for you? Do you wish to let fate take its course with no input from you? If your answer is "yes" to *any* of these questions, it's time for further self-examination. Please, take a few moments to answer these questions:

- Why do I believe I'm incapable of making my own decisions?
- What would be so bad if I made my own decision and made a mistake?
- If I don't decide for myself *now*, when will I?

Postponing decision-making may make sense if you need more information or you want to speak with someone whose opinion you value. But it's not a good idea to avoid making a decision because you're afraid to do it. For example, if you want to consult with a professor or trusted friend *before* you choose your dissertation topic, fine. But, be honest with yourself. Are you seeking additional input so that you'll be more comfortable with your decision? Or, has your confidence collapsed and you simply want someone else to make the decision for you?

Reflect on What's Exciting about a Challenge.

It's a fine line between feeling excited and feeling nervous. As a worrier, you're in the habit of leaning toward the nervous side. To counteract this tendency, deliberately lean the other way. Focus on what's exciting, stimulating, and inspiring about a challenge. As you make this shift, you'll discover that worrying and excitement have much in common. One major difference, however, is *how you interpret your mind and body experience*. So next time you have "butterflies in your stomach," interpret it as *a sign of excitement*, not fear.

If this feels counterintuitive to you, take your cue from a kid learning to ride a bike. At the beginning, the skill seems impossible to master. You're scared. You think you'll never learn how to ride. Someone must help you keep your balance or training wheels do the job for you. But then one day with enough practice, you feel ready. You're a bit wobbly but so what? It doesn't stop you; you're ready to go. No more training wheels. No more need for an adult to prop you up. You're on your own. And will you succeed? Oh yes, yes indeed! If a child can get *excited* about a challenge that initially seems scary, so can you!

Reward Yourself for Taking a Risk.

If you're having second thoughts about taking a risk, instead of backtracking or berating yourself, (e.g. I must have been crazy to join the drama club), reward yourself. One way to get on the 'this is a good idea' track is to remind yourself *why* you initially thought it was a good idea. Maybe there's a budding actor inside of you yearning to be free.

Even accomplished actors like **Katherine Hepburn** admitted to being fearful *and* doing it anyway:

> *"Everyone thought I was bold and fearless*
> *even arrogant, but inside I was always quaking."*

If one day in a burst of confidence you commit to taking on a tough assignment, don't drop the project just because you're feeling flustered about the work. Instead, stay tuned to the full range of benefits that this venture may have for you – not the least of which will be an enhanced belief in your abilities. The bottom line: rather than maximizing your worries and minimizing your competence, switch it around. *Maximize your competence* and *minimize your worries*. You'll then be on the road to developing a braver, bolder you!

Avoid Making Challenges Scarier Than They Are.

If taking on a challenge frightens you, stop. Remind yourself that academic challenges are a part of college life; they're *not* potential disasters. Yes, a tough task will require time, work, energy, concentration and perhaps assistance from others. But who said college was going to be easy? If it were, it wouldn't be valuable nor would your degree be worth much. Instead of frightening yourself, tell yourself you're in school to learn, work hard, have fun, develop new skills and enjoy new experiences.

Guard against *overestimating the time* you'll need to devote to a task, *overestimating the energy* you'll need to expend on a task, *overestimating problems* that may arise. Instead, make an objective assessment of what you'll need to do to accomplish your work. Be optimistic. If you're not weighed down by worries, it'll be easier to discover ways to make a project easier and more enjoyable. Let your new mantra be, *"I can do it!"*

Be Your Own Best Friend.

Your first impulse may be to turn to others for encouragement and support. Good! It's terrific that you have supportive people in your life. But don't let that prevent you from *turning to yourself* for encouragement. If you're frequently texting home to ask your parents how to handle a situation, you're reinforcing your dependency on them. If you keep conferring with friends about how to do a project before you even come up with your own ideas, you're reinforcing your dependency on them. In effect, you're saying, "I can't do this by myself." Such a statement minimizes your competence, creating an increasingly fragile future for you.

Yes, it's good if family and friends are there for you, helping you out *if* you need it. Hence don't cut yourself off from outside help. But do resist the temptation to turn to others *before* you turn to yourself. To fortify self-reliance, ask yourself questions such as:

- What are *my* options?
- What would *I* like to do?
- What resources might *I* explore before asking for another's input?
- What do *I* already know about this subject?

Asking yourself these questions will clarify your thinking. Then if you do seek input from others, you won't come across as weak (*I can't do this*) but as strong (*I'd appreciate your input about my ideas*). Encouraging and supporting yourself is especially important when you're feeling down. For example, if you received a lower-than-expected grade, rather than beating yourself up take a sober look at what went wrong. Learn from your mistakes.

Cultivate your inner resources. And believe what **Eleanor Roosevelt** believed:

> *"People grow through experience*
> *if they meet life honestly and courageously.*
> *This is how character is built."*

Make a Clear Commitment to Your Goals.

If you're wishy-washy about your commitments, it'll be harder for you to achieve your goals. It'll be like having one foot in the door, one foot out the door. So first, commit. Then, let that awesome brain of yours focus on *how* to achieve it. For example, if you're not fully committed to getting a graduate degree but only "thinking about it," hang-ups and bang-ups will thwart you before you even get out of the starting gate. So many roadblocks: high expenses, harsh competition, demanding courses. On the other hand, if you're seriously committed to the goal, you'll find a way to achieve it. Though you'll undoubtedly bump up against obstacles, they won't stop you.

Listen to the difference between these two statements:

- "I'd like to go to grad school, but it's so expensive and time consuming."
- "Grad school is so expensive and time consuming, but I definitely want to go."

Hear the pessimism in the first sentence; the optimism in the second sentence? Hear the reason why it's *not* likely to happen in the first sentence; the determination to *make it happen* in the second sentence?

Once you've made a serious commitment to your goal, you can then explore "how to" options. Here are a few ways to finance your education that readily come to mind:

- Work first, save money and then go to grad school.
- Work for a company that will pay (at least, in part) for your education.
- Apply for financial aid and/or scholarship grants.
- Research opportunities for Work-Study.
- Explore graduate programs overseas that may be less expensive.

Let's Get Going!

Think about a goal you'd like to achieve that's making you anxious. Now, open up a document. Give it a jazzy name. Imagine at least three ways you might move forward with this goal - despite your anxiety. Write down your ideas no matter how far-fetched they may seem. Come on; don't give up! Think outside the box. Avoid automatically naysaying any idea that pops up in your mind.

Give it a full week's time. Next week, open the document. Look at it again. What do you think? Are you pleased? Are you thinking this just might work? Reflect on *additional ways* to achieve your goal. Elaborate on the how-to until it sounds quite feasible to you. Congratulations! You're already on the right track. You're developing *an active mindset* to aid you in accomplishing your ambitions. That mindset is half the battle!

SPEAKING A New Narrative!

Limit Your Qualifiers.

Qualifiers are words like, *"maybe," "perhaps," "sort of," "kind of," "try to."* Notice how often you use them to make tentative statements – ones that dodge firm commitments. Then, start speaking more definitively.

Instead of saying, *"Maybe* I'll work on my report this week," say *"I will* work on my report this week." To enhance your effectiveness add a specific timeline, such as *"I'll* start my report on *Tuesday,* finish it by *Friday."* Give the slip to slippery statements. Aim for precision. Then, keep your word! When you break a promise to others, you're telling them they can't count on you. Breaking a promise to yourself means you can't count on yourself. That's disrespectful! Come on, I know you can do better.

End "I Can't" Sentences with "BUT One Thing I Can Do is..."

The phrase "I can't..." may leave you feeling hopeless and helpless. You've got no power, no potency, no punch; you're screwed. Rather than remaining in this defeatist position, shift the focus away from what you *can't* do to what you *can* do. For example, instead of complaining, "I can't do this statistic homework," be upbeat by adding:

- *"BUT one thing I can do is* consult with a friend who's a math whiz."
- *"BUT one thing I can do* is go online to find a tutorial to assist me."
- *"BUT one thing I can do is* speak to my professor to see if he'll clarify a few points."

Let's Get Going!

It's time to put the above advice into practice. *Write down a sentence* that begins with *"I can't."* Now, make it a compound sentence by adding, *".... BUT one thing I can do is ...."* Do it; don't just read about it! I can tell you with absolute certainty that the more you *do* the exercises in this book, the more you'll learn. Once again, notice that what comes after the BUT is what counts. Now challenge yourself to put this skill into practice!

Create an Upbeat Ending to "I Don't Know" Sentences.

Another way of encouraging yourself to become less worried is to minimize the times you say *"I don't know."* Tossing off such a statement is easy. Focusing on what you *do* know is harder. Why always settle for the easy option? To shift the focus away from what you *don't know*, add an upbeat ending. An example: *"I don't know how to do this assignment,"*

- *"BUT one thing I do know is* I can go online to research the topic."
- *"BUT one thing I do know is* I'll speak with the TA before I begin."
- *"BUT one thing I do know is* I'll get a good night's sleep. In the morning, I'll be more creative."

Making an action-oriented statement *strengthens* your resolve; making a helpless-oriented statement *weakens* your resolve. Make your choice!

Let's Get Going!

Now, it's time to make *this* tip more personal. Write down a sentence that begins with *"I don't know."* Keep the same sentence and add, *"BUT one thing I do know is ...."*

Not another exercise? Yup, another one; it won't take too long, so do it! If you're skipping over the exercises, it may well be that passivity is your biggest enemy. So, be active! Once you've expanded your sentence, what did you notice? Did you feel more empowered? More ready to take action instead of giving in to inertia? Now, challenge yourself to put this new skill into practice.

Answer "What if?" Questions.

"What if?" questions are often used by worriers to justify dragging their feet. An example: You might delay applying for a summer internship by saying, "What if I can't afford to live on what it pays?" Tell yourself this and you've hit a dead end - unless you *answer* the question! So, let's answer the question instead of amplifying your worries.

Yes, it's frustrating that internships pay so little or nothing at all. Yet, inspiration is often born from frustration. So, get inspired! Curb your impulse to give up. Instead, figure out what to do if you can't afford to live on what an internship pays. Here are a few possibilities:

- I'm starting an austerity budget today.
- I have loads of stuff I can sell on EBay to raise money.
- I'll create a pitch for my parents to see if they'll subsidize me.
- I can make good money as a dog walker for residents in the nearby community.

I've given you four prospects that might resolve your dilemma. Now it's time for you to think of *four more* and add them to the list. Then give yourself a high five for becoming a problem solver!

I'm Waiting.... Sentences need a Frisky Finale.

Waiting for something to happen may seem like a valid excuse for procrastinating. Do any of these examples feel familiar to you?

- *"I'm waiting* to see how I did on my midterm before I crack open the books again."
- "*I'm waiting* for a book to be returned to the library before I proceed with my report."
- "*I'm waiting* until the weekend to write my term paper."

Don't let *"waiting"* linger around without adding a *"meanwhile I'm doing"* clause.

- *"I'm waiting* to see how I did on my midterm; *meanwhile I'm studying for my bio exam."*
- *"I'm waiting* for a book to be returned to the library; *meanwhile, I'm revising my outline."*
- *"I'm waiting* until the weekend to write my paper; *meanwhile I'm finishing up my art project."*

Do you notice how action-oriented the second set of sentences are, how passive the first set are? Do you truly wish to wait and worry? Or, would you prefer to cultivate a "get up and go" mentality to meet your responsibilities?

ACTION Strategies!

Break up Large Tasks into Smaller Ones.

Worry has its way of intimidating you from the moment you wake up till the time you go to bed. You think about everything you need to do. OMG, it's all too much! It's so much easier to stay in bed. Stop that worrying; it's debilitating. Instead, divide the whole panorama of responsibilities into bite-size pieces so they'll be less intimidating, easier to execute. Follow this strategy:

- Specify the date by which the project needs to be completed.
- Outline the major steps you'll need to take.
- Break each step down into bite-sized pieces.
- Focus on only one step at a time.
- When you finish that step, pat yourself on the back.
- Move on to the next step.
- Then the next step.

- Monitor your progress.
- I'm 20% done, 40% done, halfway there, almost there!
- YES, I'M DONE!

An example: Composing a professional looking resume can be intimidating. Once you outline the major steps, however, it won't seem so daunting. Here's a model:

- Search online for prototypes of resumes.
- Compile a list of your previous jobs (paid and volunteer).
- Jot down descriptions of your skills.
- Compose a first draft of a resume based on the above.
- Revise that draft.
- Show your revised draft to 3 people whose opinion you respect.
- Revise the draft again.
- Produce the final copy.

Completing each small task is empowering. When you feel empowered, it increases your motivation. When you're motivated, it all gets easier. Why? Because *nothing succeeds like success!*

Use Motivational Prompts.

There are many expressions that encourage you to take action - despite your worries. Here are a few suggestions:

Short Affirmations
*You can do it! ** You're kicking butt! ** Awesome, you finished the first part!*

Motivational Book
"Oh, the Places You'll Go!" by Dr. Seuss. This is a kid's book that speaks to the scared, helpless child inside each one of us. If you read the book as a kid, read it again with a mature brain. I bet it'll help you gain the courage to act despite your fears.

Motivational Song
"Three Little Birds" by Bob Marley. *"Don't worry about a thing, 'cause every little thing's gonna be all right."* Hearing these words sung repetitively with the Marley beat reverberating in your brain is a perfect antidote for worriers - especially if you let your body move with the beat!

Let's Get Going!

Now it's time for you to collect your own motivational affirmations, books and songs. Choose ones that will flatten your fears, lift your mood and get you moving! This is not fluff; this is a genuine remedy for alleviating your fears. So get your butt moving and do it!

Seek Out Optimistic, Hopeful People.

At times, you'll need to seek advice, approval or assurance from others. When you do, be selective in whom you choose. If you seek support from an encouraging professor, you'll become more motivated, encouraged and excited about your work. If you seek support from a discouraging professor, you'll become dispirited, disheartened and discouraged with yourself and the work you need to do.

The same is true for friends. So, make sure your friends are encouraging, enthusiastic people. And whatever pessimistic, doom and gloom people are in your life, keep them at a distance. They'll be more of a liability to you than an asset. As you cultivate more positive relationships, let their confidence and courage rub off on you. Then wean yourself off of any reliance you have on pessimistic people. You don't need them to amplify your worries!

Take Action, Despite Your Discomfort.

You won't get any better at doing something if you keep avoiding it. So, expand your comfort zone by engaging in a *broader* range of activities, even if you do them awkwardly. Here are activities that students frequently steer clear of:

- Speaking in front of a group
- Asserting oneself in relationships
- Taking a leadership role in a group activity
- Admitting that you don't understand something

Don't let comfort be your primary concern. You can be uncomfortable- and do it anyway! Each activity you attempt doesn't have to be a major triumph. Keep stacking up small challenges and watch them add up to hefty accomplishments you'll be proud of!

Let's Get Going!

To gain courage and confidence, don't shy away from doing what's difficult. Every week, make a goal to initiate an action - despite your discomfort. Don't wait for a pressured situation - make it happen now! Sometimes it helps to do something spontaneously so you don't have time to talk yourself out of it. For example, maybe you're upset with a friend who often undermines what you say. You've wanted to confront him for a long time, yet *fear weakens your resolve*. Instead of planning a confrontation, just let it happen! Yes, that's tough to do. Yet, *doing something out of character helps build your character*.

Catch up on Pursuits You've Wanted to Do.

You may think that it's only onerous tasks procrastinators drag their feet on. Yet it can also be activities that are no big deal or that are truly enjoyable. Hence it's a good idea for you to get into the habit of doing one long postponed activity each week. It might be academic work, organizational work or recreation and relaxation. Not only will you be catching up on unfinished business, you'll also be creating a less pressured existence for yourself.

The task you choose needn't be a big, complicated, fearsome one. It could be something small but significant, like deleting old computer files, reconnecting with a friend or cleaning out that messy drawer. You might even do something just for fun that you haven't done for weeks, like play the guitar or sketch a picture. Don't judge yourself by how well you do these things, *just do them.*

GUIDED IMAGERY
Relax and Let Go!

Instead of worrying, wouldn't it be awesome if you could cultivate an opposing frame of mind: one that's confident, courageous and optimistic? The following guided imagery will steer you in that direction.

Choose a comfortable place to sit that's quiet, dimly lit and free from distractions. Take a few deep breaths to relax your body, s-l-o-w-l-y inhaling through your nose, then s-l-o-w-l-y exhaling through your mouth. Let go of any tension or tightness in your body. Allow the thoughts and cares of the day to drift away, leaving your body light, your mind empty.

Read each section of the visualization slowly, pausing for about 20 seconds between each instruction. Or, have someone else read it to you so you can close your eyes, relax and let your mind just be. Let's begin!

Picture yourself in a densely wooded forest at the edge of a clearing. As you look around, you notice that there are only a few gaps between the trees; hence it's tough for you to see what's ahead. Though you thought it would be fun to take a stroll through the forest, *your body refuses to move.* It's tightened up, becoming rigid and still. Feel the tension in your arms, legs and torso. Notice that your breathing is now heavy.

Suddenly, you hear a *soft* voice in the forest *gently* calling your name. As it continues to call, you feel your body becoming calmer, your mind more serene. Hear the voice getting stronger. Suddenly, you recognize that it's *your own voice,* yet sounding much more confident than you usually sound.

The voice stops. Then several yards into the forest, you see someone coming toward you. It's too shadowy to make out who it is. But as the person moves to the edge of the clearing, you see that this figure is *you* but you appear *more self-assured* than you usually are. Notice what makes you look so confident.

See the new you walk into the clearing and stop in front of you. Imagine feeling completely at ease with both parts of yourself standing face-to-face. Hear your confident self say, *"You can move out of your comfort zone. I'll be there to catch you if you fall. I'll show you the way forward if you're lost."*

Savor these words. Relish the hope they give you. Feel confidence rising in your body. Feel warmth spreading from your heart. Then, imagine yourself *walking forward into the forest,* knowing that the more confident you will be there to back you up with support and strength.

As you walk through the forest, notice that the trees have become less dense, allowing the sun to shine through. You walk until the forest opens up into a meadow. You gaze up at the clear blue sky. You're feeling brave and bold. You've gained the courage and confidence to go forward and look fear in the face so that it no longer intimidates you! Stay with this feeling.

Notice how relaxed you feel – in body and mind. Take as much time as you need before you return to the present. Still keeping your body relaxed, reflect on three tasks you can do, now that you're feeling more confident. Write down what you're thinking. Then, get moving. If you wish, record the instructions so you can play them back at a later date to see what new imagery comes to mind.

What's Your Next Step?

Congratulations! You've completed the program for worriers. Now take a moment to simply relax and breathe deeply. I hope you don't feel overwhelmed by all the valuable information in this chapter. Yes, you can read it all, but you can't absorb it all - at least not right away.

So, return to the change program and choose no more than *three skills you PROMISE yourself you'll implement NOW*. Learning these skills is a prerequisite for outsmarting your procrastination. But it's not just learning them; it's putting them into practice and retaining them. You'll do that, right?

I hope you remember what I said at the beginning of the change program. It's designed to be *a reference* for you. So, take in what you can use now. Then when you're ready, return to the program to see what's next for you. Just don't wait too long!

Never forget that your personality style has many great qualities. You're caring, conscientious and concerned about your future. Excellent! Now make sure your worries don't stop you from being all you can be! Use the skills you just learned to tone down your worries, rev up your excitement and live a larger life.

Now might be a good time to take a short break. Get up and stretch. Do some sit-ups. Grab a snack. If it's cookie dough ice cream, would you save some for me - please? Then move on to the next chapter to continue your journey. There's a lot more to learn.

"The greatest mistake you can make in life
is to be continually fearing you'll make one."
~**Elbert Hubbard**

CHAPTER 7

THE CRISIS-MAKER
...BUT I WORK BEST UNDER PRESSURE!

Welcome Crisis-Makers! You have many exceptional qualities. You thrive on excitement. You enjoy action and adventure. You respond well in an emergency when everyone else is losing their heads. So what could be wrong?

It's those unnecessary crises you create by not paying attention to assignments till the last minute. Those rushed reports and narrow escapes from impending deadlines take its toll. This chapter will help you gain a better understanding of your crisis-maker personality and how it holds you back from being all you can be.

What are some of the telltale signs of being a crisis-maker procrastinator? Here's a mini-version of the quiz you took earlier. See if these questions resonate with you:

- Does my motivation to work change quickly and dramatically?
- Am I easily seduced into responding to the need of the moment?
- Do I ignore assignments, then work frantically at the last minute to get them done?

"I work best under pressure!" is the battle cry of the crisis-maker procrastinator. You may proclaim it proudly, intimating that you have special last minute "rush to the rescue" capabilities. Or, you may utter it sheepishly recognizing that any skill you have in coping with emergencies is not a special ability but a necessary evil generated by creating the crisis in the first place. The bottom line for both the proud and the sheepish is that no matter how much you justify your MO, you can't escape the fact that you're addicted to the adrenaline rush of doing things at the last moment. Until you experience that rush, it's tough for you to get your butt moving.

If you're a crisis-maker, you know your life often resembles a roller coaster ride. First you sit back waiting for the action that'll get your adrenaline flowing. Before long, you're jerked into an exciting, energizing high! Once the high has passed, you fall back into dreary inaction. Your two operating modes are: burying your head in the sand, then working frantically when you're under the gun. You may believe that you have no control over this pattern. It's just the way you operate - shrug. Nope, it doesn't have to be that way. Stay with me, won't you? I've got ideas for you that will enhance your life. Promise!

Two Crisis-Maker Styles

Now it's time for me to introduce you to two crisis-makers who are allowing their crises to crush their confidence.

Proud Crisis-Maker

Wayne often boasts about his heroic crisis-maker style as he musters up the energy to get stuff done at the 11th hour. He claims to like the challenge of doing things at the last minute and it's not just his school work he's referring to. If Wayne is meeting friends for dinner, he thinks nothing of leaving at the last minute to get there on time – or not. If he needs to catch a train, he plays a "seat of the pants" game: leaving late, gambling that there'll be no traffic, wagering that he'll find a quick parking spot at the station. "It's a game," he admits. "I get to the station on time or I curse myself out because I've blown it. It sounds stupid, I know, but it makes my life more captivating. I hate doing stuff in a tedious, tiresome way."

Though Wayne tells himself he wants to get his work done on time, he wastes huge blocks of time doing nothing productive. He admits to having trouble getting going until he's under the gun. Comparing himself to his older brother, he says, "I admire his ways but I could never be like him. He's so predictable; that's not me!" Wayne believes that his problem is a lack of willpower. That's undoubtedly true. But underlying his lack of willpower is a habit of letting the thrill of a self-made crisis become his major motivator to get moving.

Humbled Crisis-Maker

Lori is also a crisis-maker but instead of being boastful about it, she's down on herself, acknowledging how often her procrastination has resulted in lower grades, lost opportunities and labored relationships. Lori was raised in a family where both parents were alcoholic; hence she feels that she has never had much control over her life. She views herself as a bit ditzy, doomed to be out of sync with the world. She can't help delaying, ignoring or even totally forgetting what she was going to do until a crisis sets in. Then she becomes hysterical, running around frantically trying to get it all done. "I'm an awful planner," Lori admits. "I wait till the last minute to do my homework even though I know I won't have enough time to do a great job. When I'm finally down to the wire, I go crazy trying to get it all done. I blame myself; I blame others; I whimper; I whine. At those moments, my self-esteem is in the toilet."

Lori recognizes how dysfunctional her pattern is but when it comes to changing her ways, she just shrugs it off believing there's no way she can change. Like Wayne, her last minute decision-making affects more than her academic life. It's typical for her to wait until the last minute to decide what to wear. Describing one such incident, she said, "I was frantically searching through my closet. I threw together one outfit, yanked it on, yanked it off, then went on to the next one. Soon my bed looked like a bomb hit it. I started screaming in frustration. My roommate shocked me when she said. 'You're out-of-control! You gotta get help!' She's right but I can't change." Lori's wrong. She's capable of learning new strategies and skills that will enable her to respond in a more modulated manner.

Four Crisis-Maker Traits

Have to get Hyped BEFORE Taking Action

It's the pressure of the approaching deadline that finally gets crisis-makers moving. This is especially true when they've got a task to do that they're not interested in. And let's face it; that includes many academic assignments. Until the moment of doom plops down on their doorstep, they don't budge. They claim, without an iota of logic, that there's nothing to get excited about; there's plenty of time to do it. Then, when time is running out they jump into action with a big burst of energy.

Wayne, for example, approaches his schoolwork as a game, seeing no point putting in time writing papers or studying for exams until a deadline is staring him in the face. Lori simply doesn't plan. Instead, she counts on last minute hysteria to provide the momentum needed to carry her through. Since pandemonium was a frequent occurrence in her childhood, she's used to it, viewing it as nothing out of the ordinary.

Momentary Feelings Rule

Why do crisis-makers get going only when there's a blazing fire to put out? Because their feelings at the moment rank high. If they don't *feel* like doing something, they won't. If they *feel* an undertaking isn't to their liking, they don't reflect on why it still may be a good idea to do it. Crisis-makers find it tough to respond to tasks in a thoughtful, practical, and efficient manner. No crisis, no need to act. When others urge them to act with more immediacy, their typical retort is, why would I do it now when I can do it later?

We see this characteristic in Wayne's insistence that he can't tackle tasks if he doesn't *feel* like doing it. He's convinced that it would simply be too tedious for him to alter his pattern even though he's never given it a fair chance. Lori believes she can't give up her addiction to living a frenetic life, despite the fact that her turbulent existence makes her miserable. It's as if she's afraid that without one crisis after another, she'd be left in a state of lethargy. She's unaware that the two states - crisis and lethargy - are co-dependent and that a different state of well-balanced efficiency is preferable to either one of them.

Drawn to Drama

Crisis-makers are drawn toward the theatrical. Lucky for them, procrastination provides them with all the dramatic elements they'll ever need. There's conflict: the hero is challenged with a taxing task. There's suspense: will the hero get the task done? And there's a thrilling climax: victory against all odds or demeaning defeat.

Wayne represents the fully flamboyant hero. He courts disaster by letting things go until the last minute, not only as a way of making life more riveting to him but also as a way of making him more riveting to others. We can imagine his friends sitting in that restaurant waiting for him to make his grand entrance, wondering "Will he get here? Did something happen to him? What's his excuse going to be this time?" Though Lori's not trying to be a hero by procrastinating, it does provide a way for her to get attention. Consider the time she was trying on outfits for a party. She wound up crying out in frustration, a signal for her roommate to calm her down and provide a summation of her performance!

Craves Attention

Underneath many crisis-makers' theatrics is a craving for attention and importance. This is easily procured by stirring up dramatic scenarios, which procrastination easily does. They hope to shock themselves not only into *doing something* but also into *being someone*. Not just an ordinary person, but the central figure in a drama.

Wayne exhibits this characteristic by delaying doing almost anything until he has a chance to do it heroically, that is, in the fastest time possible. It's a big crap shoot but it's the only way he knows how to jumpstart his engine. Crises enable Lori to escape her despondent feelings with a frenzy of self-display. She runs around, gets hysterical and screams for help. Far from being a hopeless non-entity with no control over her life, she loops into being a bombastic "wild woman!"

Zach's Journey from CRISIS-MAKING to DECISION-MAKING!

Zach, a 21-year-old economics major, introduced himself to me as an 11th-hour specialist. With a grin on his face, he said, "I like that moniker. I admit, however, that at times I wonder what the hell am I doing? Why do I keep letting myself fall into the same do-or-die syndrome?" When I asked Zach to describe what he meant, he said, "I don't get moving 'til the last minute. Then once I'm in the zone, a wave of energy courses through my body. I'm on a roll - ready to tackle anything that needs to be done!"

I asked Zach to tell me what his feelings are before he's in the zone. "To be honest," he shrugged, "I don't feel much of anything. Yeah, there's work to do but I can't bring myself to care about it. I just want to play video games, strum my guitar. You name it; any alternative seems more desirable."

Zach admitted that his moods change dramatically – from the high of being in the zone to the low of not caring about what needs to be done. This emotional seesaw was his primary motivation for seeking coaching. "Lately, it's harder for me to swing into action at the last minute," he confessed. "What used to be exciting now feels like an ordeal. After pulling an all-nighter, I'm wiped out and disappointed in myself for creating this chaos."

Zach wanted to alter his pattern, viewing it as too risky to dismiss with a cocky attitude. Though he was a senior in college, he still had two incompletes to make up. He had also failed a course that he wanted to repeat to raise his GPA. His 'F', he claimed, had not been earned; it had come by default as he never applied for a withdrawal in a timely manner. "Sometimes when I'm late with a task, I simply ignore it," Zach fessed up. "I go into my 'oh well, whatever' mode. I know I should be more concerned about some stuff but it's easy for me to just shrug my shoulders. My dad's on my case though; he's giving me hell. His frustration with me will finally force me to finish my work."

Zach was brought up in a loving family with parents who had always been there to bail him out. As good as their intentions were, however, they'd inadvertently reinforced his negative habits. The end result: he believed he didn't have to be responsible until he "grew up" – which increasingly became sometime in the future. "I confess, I'm spoiled," Zach chuckled. "I was brought up in a family where Dad worked long hours and Mom was a stay-at-home mom, always there to help me and my brother when we needed it. Coming from this background, I vowed to never work as hard as my dad. It's not worth it. I'm going to have as much fun as I can."

When Zach was in junior high, he was diagnosed with ADD (attention deficit disorder). Because of this, his mom was more than willing to work with him to make sure he got his homework done. "Mom was very well organized," he recalled. "She'd sit me down at the dining room table to do my homework and work with me until I was finished. She'd go online to get what I needed and clipped stuff I could use from the newspaper. I'd be chomping at the bit to get out of doing the work. I wanted to do something else, anything else, but she pressured me until I did what I was supposed to do. Every day she'd lecture me, 'Work now, then you'll be free to do whatever you want. You'll feel better when your work is done.' But I didn't see things that way. 'Take your tomorrow,' I'd tell her. 'I want today; I want to be happy now!'"

Now that Zach was in college, his mother was no longer able to *make* him do his homework. Nevertheless, he usually had someone around who would prod him into action. During the time I knew him, the prodder was his girlfriend, Gina. "We bonded over our differences - her studying, me going out. I pushed her to go out (which she loved) and she pushed me to study (which I ignored). Now Gina's upset that she does more for me than I do for her. She's right. I say I'll change and I do. But I have to admit, I keep reverting back to my old ways."

Zach was no dummy. He was aware of the parallel between how he responded to his relationships and to his academic work. With work assignments, he'd repeatedly let things drift along until a crisis developed. Then he'd work at a hero's pace, get stuff done and the crisis would pass. After that, he'd let things drift along once again. Sometimes, however, the crisis didn't pass without consequences: a low grade, an incomplete, a lost opportunity. Zach would let even maintenance chores turn into crises before he got around to dealing with them. "I neglect to take care of my car," he admitted, "until it's an emergency. Last week, the motor was overheating. I knew it needed oil for weeks. Yet, I waited for a crisis to develop before I took action."

As for Zach's academic career, his lifelong habit of procrastination was coming to a head. He doubted whether he'd ever achieve success unless he made major changes. Although he acted nonchalant, he did want to graduate on time and even go on to get his MBA. To do the latter, he knew he had to study for the GMATs. But every time he sat down to study, his mind wandered. Often he'd drink a few beers, thinking that might settle him down. But then he was too tired to focus on anything. "I know now," he admitted, "that if I don't change my habits, my habits will ruin my future."

Zach was right. Crisis-maker patterns typically evolve into larger problems after college for two reasons. Pulling an all-nighter becomes harder the older you are, especially when the next day you need to be at work and no longer have the luxury of catching up on your zzz's. And once you're employed, procrastination affects not only *your* performance but also your colleagues. If they're waiting around for your work to be done before they can complete theirs, repercussions abound!

Zach's First Steps Forward:

Zach kicked off his change program by modifying one of his most noticeable mannerisms, speaking in highly dramatic language. A night out was *"the best ever"* or *"the pits."* A course was either *"sensational"* or *"a complete waste of time."* Such speech reflected and reinforced his crisis-maker ways.

Instead of using dramatic words for effect, Zach made a conscious effort to use more temperate language. Pretty soon, he became aware that he didn't have to utter the first words that popped into his head! He could think before he spoke. This change happened so fast, he was shocked. Shocked not only that he could change but that his words influenced his mood and actions. After a lifetime of crisis-making - *stupid, stupid, stupid,* he muttered, Zach flipped the script and began working on assignments *before* time was running out.

Your Change Program
from CRAZED to COMPOSED!

Creating new habits isn't easy but it also isn't as hard as you might imagine. Not if you do it step by step - even baby step by baby step. As you read this chapter, you'll learn many ways to help you overcome your procrastination. However, I *don't* want you to do them all. Try and you'll become overwhelmed.

Hence, once you've finished this chapter, return to this page and scroll through the ideas I've gifted you. Then choose no more than *three skills that you PROMISE yourself you'll implement NOW*. Take on too much and it's likely you'll crash, creating more chaos for yourself.

I've designed this change program to be *a reference* for you. Thus once you've got a few skills under your belt, *return for more*. Just don't wait too long! Now, let's delve into specific strategies to help you curb your crisis-making patterns.

Once they become part of your routine, your life will be far less chaotic. Are you ready to begin your journey? Great! I'm psyched. Hope you are too!

THINKING To Get You Moving!

Work Time? Put the Executive Part of Your Brain in Charge.

Rather than letting your desires, distractions and last-minute deadlines decide what you'll do, make sure the executive (smart) part of your brain is head honcho. All the time? No, not all the time, but when it's work time - YES! The emotional part of your brain may insist that assignments have to be exciting to lure you into action. Tell the emotional part to back off! Then, let the executive part coach you into adopting a more active, upbeat approach.

Often it's the first few minutes of doing a task that's the major obstacle. An example: You may not want to go to the gym, yet once you're there you feel energized! So, instead of letting your whims, distractions and emergencies decide what you'll do, let your executive self decide. Instead of thinking "an assignment has to interest me before I do it," think "I have to start doing an assignment before it interests me." Please no eye-rolling; this approach really works. Perhaps you remember when you were a little kid and were made to take a bath. You didn't want to but once you were in the tub, you didn't want to get out!

Focus on the Facts, Not on Your Feelings.

As a crisis-maker, you're inclined to put more emphasis on how you *feel*, less emphasis on what you *know*. Feelings are important, of course. But so are thoughts. Hence, strive toward a *viable* balance of the two. When it's time to take care of your responsibilities, shift your focus *away* from your feelings. Then focus on doing what needs to be done *despite* your feelings. Here are two examples of how your feelings might get you in trouble:

- My report's due on Wednesday (fact) but I can make up an excuse and hand it in on Friday (feeling).
- My gas gauge is on empty (fact) but there's plenty of gas to get me there (feeling).

Focus on the facts. Then rejoice when you notice that your assumptions mesh up with reality!

Reflect on WHY it's a Good Idea to do Your Work Early.

Instead of relying on last minute stress to be your major motivator, let positive passions inspire you to *do* your work. Here are 8 questions to ask when tempted to put off doing a task:

- Will being a self-starter make me feel better about myself?
- Will doing my work develop my independence and maturity?
- Will doing my work earlier make it feel less burdensome?
- Will finishing this task give me more time to do other things?
- Will doing my work improve my relationship with others (i.e. teachers, friends, family)?
- Will doing my work in a timely way benefit me or my parents financially?
- Will doing my work enhance my sense of accomplishment or career prospects?
- Will doing my work fulfill my curiosity about a topic?

"At a child's birth, if a mother could ask a fairy godmother to endow it with the most useful gift, that gift would be curiosity."
~Eleanor Roosevelt

Let's Get Going!

Reread the questions above. Choose at least three of them. Create a document entitled: *"Reasons to Get My Work Done on Time."* Write down thoughtful answers to your questions. Let your answers be the motivating force for you next time you're tempted to delay doing your work.

Cease Viewing Yourself as a Victim.

No, you're not a helpless victim! Sure there may be some aspects of academia that you have no control over. So what? You signed up for higher education. Hence, I assume you want to get your degree and grow your future. And yes, that invariably means doing some assignments you've no inherent interest in as well as studying some stuff you're not enthusiastic about. So, you've got one of two roads to go down.

Suck it up and do it anyway, figuring out some way to make it a more meaningful experience. Or, if much of your academic experience is truly distasteful to you, review your decision about school. After all, you're not in jail. But it might be that you're in the wrong program, the wrong college, the wrong class or working with the wrong professor. Reflect on the matter. Pinpoint the problem. Then make a decision as to how you'll continue spending your time, money and energy over the next few years. By pondering these matters, you move out of the position of helpless victim.

When you believe you have no choice in what you need to do, you reinforce a powerless mind-set. And if you don't do anything about changing *that* now, what makes you think you'll be any different when you're finished with formal schooling? Even if you're working at a job you love, there'll be some aspects of your work that you won't like. You'll need to accept it or see if there's a way to change it. One way you might view an annoying assignment with a positive, action-oriented approach is to think, "I'll suggest to my professor a different approach to writing my paper; hopefully he'll give me a thumbs up!" In contrast, if you view yourself as a powerless victim, you'll probably think, "This assignment sucks; I never get a chance to do what I want!"

> *"Everyone thinks of changing the world,*
> *but no one thinks of changing himself."*
> ~ Leo Tolstoy

SPEAKING A New Narrative!

Be Aware of Exaggerating Your Responsibilities.

Resist your tendency to add fuel to the fire by speaking about your responsibilities as bigger than they really are. Examples of such rants are: I've got a zillion assignments to do this week! All this reading is driving me crazy! Professors just pile on the work! Instead, clarify and moderate your responsibilities by speaking about them in a down-to-earth mode:

- Clarify all these things that you have to do this week.
- Choose what task you can begin to do right now.
- Talk about how you can make your obligations seem less overwhelming.

Use More Thinking Words, Fewer Feeling Words.

Using words that kick-start negativity sucks the energy out of you before you even begin. Words such as:

- I hate… I'm exhausted… I don't give a damn about… It bites to have to…

In contrast, using energizing words help motivate you to get going. Words such as:

- I'm shooting for… I'm aspiring to… I'm aiming for… I'm looking forward to…

My goal is not to turn you into a robotic nerd. Of course, you can express negative emotions. Just don't let those emotions impede you from getting down to work.

Let's Get Going!

Think about a time when you viewed yourself as a victim. If you're about to skip this exercise by saying, *"This is dumb"* or *"I can't do this,"* you're enacting the victim position. So instead of complaining, do the exercise! Remember what you said to yourself that made you feel victimized or powerless. Now, think about how you could have gained power. This may have been the power to speak up, take action, or tell yourself, *"I won't be a victim."* The answer may not pop into your head right away but stay with it.

In *every* situation, you've got power. Don't believe me? Here's what **Viktor Frankel,** a World War II concentration camp survivor said:

> *"The one thing you can't take away from me*
> *is the way I choose to respond to what you do to me."*

Think about that!

Play Up the Positive Aspects of a Task.

Now that you've stopped speaking about yourself as a victim, you have stopped, haven't you?, it's also a good idea to stop bad-mouthing your responsibilities. It may be tempting to speak about what you need to do as dire, devastating, even disastrous. But it's certainly not helpful! For example, if you have an obligation to fill out a financial aid form, you may hone in on "how difficult and time-consuming" the task is. Keep speaking about it that way and it'll be a prescription for procrastination.

I'm not suggesting you lie about how you feel. Expressing a negative feeling is fine as long as *you follow up* with an upbeat, action-oriented ending to your sentence. Here are two examples:

- "I hate filling out this form *BUT it's in my best interest to do it.*"
- "This financial aid form is so time-consuming *BUT when I finish it, I'll get my tuition aid for next year - yippee!*"

Once you develop a habit of ending your sentences on an upbeat note, it'll be much easier to focus your attention on what you can do to *improve* your situation. I hope you have nothing against that!

Avoid Using Dramatic Language.

Dramatic language encourages the emotional part of your brain to take over, relegating the executive part of your brain to the trash bin. If you hate the assignment your professor gave you, you might describe it as *"asinine"* or *"absurd."* If you don't agree with your coach's advice, you might describe it as *"senseless"* or *"stupid."*

If this is what you say to yourself, it's going to be next to impossible for you to approach any assignment or advice in a positive way. So, counteract your tendency to use dramatic language by using more moderate words. Even when you want to express annoyance, you can still use more temperate words. I hope you can hear the difference between, *"I'm frustrated with this homework assignment"* and *"What an absurd assignment; it's a complete waste of time; I hate it!"*

ACTION Strategies!

Keep a Journal - Let's Get Going!

Keep a journal of your repetitive crises. I know, it's a pain. But it's helpful for you to become aware of *when* and *why* those crises keep popping up. So, keep your journal simple, jotting down occasions when:

- You didn't address a problem when you should have; now it's become a crisis.
- You ignored taking care of a responsibility; now others are upset with you.
- You wasted time doing nothing productive; now the deadline date is upon you.

Record the time and date for each incident, including statements about:

- What was your major procrastination trigger (i.e. hangover, bad mood, lethargy)?
- What motivated you to finally get off your butt (i.e. a full-blown crisis, a change of heart, a coach)?
- What false assumptions did you harbor (i.e. wrong deadline date, forgot a fact, didn't think it mattered)?

When you keep a journal, you'll become more aware. When you become more aware, you'll be more mindful. When you become more mindful, you'll be more attentive. When you become more attentive, you'll be more motivated to take action. This is your future we're talking about. So, get going!

Create Action Plans for the Crises in Your Journal.

After a month of keeping your journal, review what you wrote. Notice if there's a pattern to it. Here's what one crisis-maker said, "I have a tough time getting motivated when I'm alone as I feel so lethargic. But when others are around, I have FOMO, so I procrastinate then too." Once you notice a pattern to your procrastination, you can take steps to counteract it. If you know you have difficulty getting revved up in the early hours of the day, start your morning with a physical activity to get your motor running, such as:

- 20 sit-ups before you get in the shower.
- 20 minute jog to get your mind and body going.
- 20 minute clean-up campaign of your personal space.

If you know you have trouble studying when others are around, create a less distractible environment, such as:

- Find a quiet environment; the library's a great place.
- Create study time when there's no distracting activity nearby.
- Join a serious study group with people who will help you focus.

By now, you know that *no system works unless you work the system*. Experiment with different solutions until you see what works for you!

Let's Get Going!

Think of a specific task you're dragging your heels on. Then write down your answers to these questions:

- How can I *start* this task? It's often helpful to begin with the easiest or most interesting part.
- What's likely to happen if I don't take action *now*?
- How will I feel about *the task* next week if I don't do anything now?
- How will I feel about *myself* next week if I don't do anything now?
- What did I learn that I want to remember next time I'm inclined to put off tending to a task?

Motivate Yourself by Creating a Game.

Many crisis-makers have a playful nature. If that's you, capitalize on it! When faced with a boring assignment, make it exciting by creating a game that can help you get it done. Here are a few suggestions:

Play "Beat the Clock."

Set your alarm for an amount of time that will challenge you to get a task done quickly. Then work as fast as you can to complete the job! If you haven't finished, set the alarm once again and get going. This is *a self-generated mini-crisis* that gets your adrenaline going to do what needs to be done. No need for a real crisis to develop.

Organize dry study material into song lyrics.

When you were a little kid, you probably learned the alphabet by singing the "A-B-C" song. Now use your creativity to write your own song to remember details you tend to forget!

Create a clever mnemonic device to serve as a memory aid.

An example: HOMES helps you recall the names of the Great Lakes: Huron, Ontario, Michigan, Erie, Superior. Now get inspired and create a mnemonic device to help you remember procedures, theories, formulas and anything else you're required to memorize. Who knows, maybe what you invent will become textbook material!

> *"In every job that must be done, there is an element of fun.*
> *You find the fun and... SNAP! The job's a game!"*
> ~ from *"Mary Poppins"*

Participate in Competitive, Challenging Activities.

If you need an adrenaline rush to get going, don't just sit there creating a crisis. Instead, get involved in challenging activities that will do the job for you. Here are a few examples:

- Competitive sports
- Creating a comedy skit
- Post a YouTube video
- Launch a website
- Draw a caricature of a professor

There are so many activities worthy of your energy. Spending your time doing them will be more fun and more fulfilling than simply trying to survive the storm your procrastination stirs up!

GUIDED IMAGERY
Relax and Let Go!

If you're often caught up in a cycle of excitement followed by a collapse of energy, it's probably rare for you to experience *genuine peace of mind*. This guided imagery will help you appreciate the difference between the *energizing* experience of sensory balance and the *exhausting* experience of sensory overload.

Choose a comfortable place to sit that's quiet, dimly lit and free from distractions. Take a few deep breaths to relax your body, s-l-o-w-l-y inhaling through your nose, then s-l-o-w-l-y exhaling through your mouth. Let go of any tension or tightness in your body. Allow the thoughts and cares of the day to drift away, leaving your body light, your mind empty.

Read each section of the visualization slowly, pausing for about 20 seconds between each instruction. Or, have someone else read it to you so you can close your eyes, relax and let your mind just be. Let's begin!

Picture yourself in a room that's completely dark and silent. You can't see, hear, smell, touch or taste anything. Feel yourself getting nervous about what might happen in the darkness.

Suddenly, a light switches on. You see yourself standing in a room surrounded by people demanding you do what *they* want you to do. You run from person to person, noticing how upset each one is. You hear voices insisting that you do something *right now*. Feel your body getting tense, your mind becoming agitated. Chaos is swirling around you.

In the midst of the chaos, you notice a light switch on the wall. You turn the switch *off* and are plunged once again into total darkness and silence. Stay with your feelings.

In a few moments, you notice *a radiating light* in the darkness that's spotlighting a cozy, comfortable chair. You hear a calm voice saying, *"Sit down and relax. It's time for you to be soothed in all five senses."* Though you're wary, you decide to trust what the voice has told you.

As you sit comfortably in the darkness, you hear *soft, sweet music.* You hear birds singing. You hear a bubbly brook. It all feels so peaceful. Stay with your feelings.

Now the darkness is lifting. You see that it's a *bright sunny day.* You see a beautiful meadow with colorful flowers, waving grasses and small groves of trees. You notice white clouds sailing across the blue sky. The air feels refreshing as it lightly caresses your body.

You're aware that you're getting hungry. Suddenly a small table appears that holds *three of your favorite foods.* You eat until you feel pleasantly full, taking pleasure in the delicious tastes, relishing the fragrant smells.

You're feeling fully relaxed yet your body feels fully alive. Relish the feeling. You hear a gentle voice telling you, *"You can stay calm and still be productive. You can enjoy and still do all you need to do."* Take comfort in the words you've just heard. Notice how relaxed you feel – in mind and body.

Take time to absorb the meaning of your visualization before you move on to the next section. Write down what you want to remember. If you wish, record the instructions so you can play them back at a later date to see what new imagery comes to mind.

What's Your Next Step?

Congratulations! You've completed the program for crisis-makers. Now take a moment to simply relax and breathe deeply. I hope you don't feel overwhelmed by all the valuable information in this chapter. Though you can read it all, you can't absorb it all - at least not right away.

So, go back and scroll through the change program, choosing no more than *three skills that you PROMISE yourself you'll implement NOW.* Learning these skills is a prerequisite for outsmarting your procrastination. But it's not just learning them; it's putting them into practice and retaining them. You'll do that, right?

I hope you remember what I said at the beginning of the change program. It's designed to be *a reference* for you. Take in what you can use now. Then when you're ready, return to the program to see what's next for you.

Just don't wait too long!

Never forget that your personality style has many great qualities. You thrive on excitement; you enjoy action and adventure; you respond well in an emergency. Excellent! Now you've got to use those traits to advance your education rather than letting them stop you from being all you can be!

Now might be a good time to take a short break. Get up and stretch. Do a few bridges for a sculpted butt and a healthy back. Grab a snack. Is it maple walnut ice cream? If it is, save some for me; I'll be there shortly! Then move on to the next chapter to continue your journey. There's still a lot more to learn.

"Inspiration is for amateurs.
The rest of us just show up and get to work."
~ **Chuck Close**

CHAPTER 8

THE DEFIER
...BUT WHY SHOULD *I* DO IT?

Welcome Defiers! You have many enviable qualities. You're not afraid to question authority. You're self-reliant. You're brave and bold. You have no qualms about saying what you think. So what could be wrong?

There are times you're a rebel without a cause, hurting no one but yourself. This may be true whether you're openly defiant or passive-aggressive which is hiding your defiance under a guise of compliance. Or you might be a combination of the two. In this chapter, you'll learn how to stand up for yourself without working against yourself.

What are some of the telltale signs of a defier procrastinator? Here's a mini-version of the quiz you took earlier. See if these questions resonate with you.

- Do I become sulky, sarcastic or argumentative when asked to do something I don't want to do?
- Do I blow off tasks I'm expected to do, claiming I've forgotten them or that they're unimportant?
- Do I take offense when others tell me how I should do things differently?

"It is our attitude at the beginning of a difficult task which, more than anything else, will affect its successful outcome."
~ William James

Two DEFIER Styles

Now it's time for me to introduce you to two defiers whose agitation, anger and arousal are hampering their headway.

Openly Aggressive Defier

Shelly prides herself on being a fiercely independent person who doesn't need or want anyone to tell her what to do. She relishes her independence, taking pride in being a rebel, a maverick, a lone voice in the wilderness. Cherishing her autonomy, she's inclined to consider demands on her as unfair, responding with her signature complaint, *"BUT why should I do it?"* At times, she questions the importance of the task at hand, emphasizing the word '*should*'; other times she implies that the task is an unfair imposition, emphasizing the word '*I.*'

When upset, she doesn't hesitate to express herself with fighting words:

- "How could he give me such a crappy grade?"
- "She has no idea what she's talking about!"
- "He's tormenting me with that asinine assignment!"

It's not just her words that display defiance; it's also her actions. She has no regrets about petty acts of defiance, like returning library books late or neglecting to pay parking tickets. It helps us to understand Shelly's stance when we take a look at her childhood. She was raised in a family where she viewed her mother as a "doormat," her father as a "tyrant." She remembers being no more than 8 years old when she vowed to never end up in her mother's position. She wouldn't ever tolerate being constantly berated, put down or shut up.

Shelly admits to having a chip on her shoulder. Given that her thinking is dichotomous – to be dominated or to dominate - her active defiance is a no-brainer. What she has yet to learn is that there are many ways to respond to others. The choice need not be victim or persecutor.

As long as Shelly gets to call the shots, relationships work well. When others disagree, however, her retort borders on the abusive. Rather than viewing teachers as allies with whom you may disagree, she views them as controllers who threaten her personal freedom. Though Shelly's unhappy with her life, she doesn't have the slightest idea about how to improve it. Expressing righteous indignation is easy; being introspective is hard.

Passive-Aggressive Defier

Jordan views himself as a nice guy. When asked to take care of a task, he typically responds *"no problem."* However, he ends up doing the task reluctantly or simply dodges doing it altogether. Saying *yes* when your actions say *no* is no way to make friends and influence people. Indeed, inconsistencies between words and actions may create more negative vibes than openly aggressive behavior.

Jordan was raised as an only child by a single mom. In his early years, she imposed on him a rigorous schedule for doing homework and household chores. He felt she was too strict but it was easier to do things her way than to incur her disfavor. Though openly compliant, Jordan developed a defiance that detonated in adolescence. He called it his *"silent rebellion."* He'd agree to whatever his mom wanted but then do whatever he pleased. This put him in the power seat. No matter how upset his mom would get about his failure to live up to his word, there was nothing she could do about it. Her tirades had lost their power to intimidate him.

Wanting to get his mom off his back, Jordan became skilled in passive-aggressive strategies such as:

- "I'll do it in a minute, Ma." (Never giving it a second thought.)
- "I did my homework." (Only his math homework.)
- "Don't worry; I'll get it done." (Never says when.)
- "Yeah, I'll do it." (He yells, as he scoots out the door.)
- "It's not due till next week." (Puts off work until the last day.)
- "When I finish this game." (Always a reason why he can't do it *now*.)

Such behaviors are still prevalent in Jordan's life. He refuses to be pinned down to deadlines, won't negotiate a compromise and doesn't directly say no. Instead, his way of working it out with others is to agree, then do it his way or simply not do it at all.

Jordan's roommate Mark says he can't rely on anything Jordan says because he's always got an escape clause. A few of his favorites:

- I forgot!
- I didn't say I'd do it, I only said I might!
- I didn't have time!
- Quit bugging me!
- So what, it's not important!

If Mark calls Jordan on his excuses, Jordan turns the table on him saying: "Aw, come on! Why are you making such a big deal over this?" His response implies that it's Mark's fault for calling him out on such a trivial matter. Mark shakes his head in disbelief, concluding that Jordan just doesn't get it.

Jordan's career choice fits well with his rebellious mind-set, for he visualizes himself as a community agitator championing the fight for innocent victims. Only one problem: his passive-aggressive tactics are backfiring as his professors simply refuse to accept his excuses for handing in work late. Jordan's just beginning to realize how he needs to tone down his defiance before it severely damages his college experience and career goals.

Team Work

Defiers rarely appreciate how much their success is dependent upon cooperative teamwork. Though we typically think of sports teams, other teams exist. A family is a team. Indeed, when a family is termed dysfunctional, it's because they don't pull together for a common purpose the way a team should. Same goes for work groups. I hope you appreciate that you're *part of* the college team and that you don't keep yourself *apart from* the team. This doesn't mean that there's no room for disagreement. But it does mean that you don't keep bucking the system just to buck the system.

Since professors are part of the team, and not the adversary, a successful college experience requires you to acquiesce to the requirements and rules of the college. Though you may not always like the requirements, I hope you're well aware of what you're getting out of the deal: knowledge, training, enlightenment, a network of resources, a diploma, in short: an education. When professors act within their designated orbit, appreciate that it's in your best interest to accept their authority. For instance, if a chemistry professor assigns a lab project for you to do, even if you believe it's a waste of time, go along with it. If, however, the same professor tells you whom to date or how to dress, that's quite a different matter!

Four Defier Traits

Challenging Authority

Defiers become easily incensed when authority tells them what to do, interpreting such *orders* as a threat to their individuality. One way they express their agitation is to procrastinate, which is a non-violent, non-verbal way for them to say "NO!" This obviously fits the mold for passive-aggressives but even openly aggressive defiers may procrastinate when directly confronting others is too threatening. If defiers were less hostile, however, they'd feel less threatened and might even view professors as allies who can assist them in attaining their goals.

Shelly doesn't curse out professors to their face. For all her bluster, she's not that self-destructive! Instead, she rages about them to her friends, rebelling by refusing to be restrained by "artificial deadlines." Sadly, Shelly is the only real victim of her rebellion. Jordan's delaying tactics make him think he's taking a bona fide action to assert his individuality. Too bad his action is a non-action.

Seeking an Adversary

Defiers put more energy into resisting what *others* want from them, rather than focusing on what *they* want for themselves. Typically, they lack clarity about their own goals complaining that, "If you just left me alone and let me do my own thing, I'd be fine." Ironically, they're the ones who have difficulty defining their "own thing." Defiers don't stop to consider that many of the tasks they resent are what they need to do, not for others but to enhance their education and acquire the necessary tools for success. If they didn't have a chip on their shoulder, they might even enjoy tackling these allegedly "unfair tasks."

We see this characteristic in the way Shelly and Jordan express dissatisfaction with school, but have no idea what would make them feel satisfied. They've concluded that the source of their problems lies in what others do to them, not in what they do to themselves.

Lacking Focus on Their Own Behavior

Although defiers are quick to become offended by others' behaviors, they're slow to recognize how their own behavior contributes to their problems. Criticizing the criticizer is easier than taking stock of themselves. Pointing the finger at another seems particularly justified in their eyes when someone nags, scolds or finds fault with them. Too bad they don't appreciate that if they were on top of their game there'd be little need for others to be badgering them.

Shelly, the active defier, drives off friends when they dare to call her on her defiance. Jordan, the passive-aggressive, keeps himself mystified as to why he's so often "misunderstood." It simply isn't his style to question his own role in a dispute.

Easily Annoyed

Defiers view many requirements of academic life with a chip on their shoulder. Holding a grudge or grievance gives them a built-in rationale for putting things off. Requirements are "unfair," "stupid," "pointless," or _____. Fill in the blank; if you're a defier, you know your favorite gripe. Such negative thoughts undercut a positive attitude toward responsibilities, making it increasingly difficult to get down to work.

Shelly zooms in on all the things that are wrong with school, gliding over whatever may be right. In a similar fashion, Jordan views himself as the perpetually misunderstood "good guy" at the mercy of scolds who don't understand him. He's finally recognizing that his lifelong inclination toward procrastination has become so potentially ruinous that he's ready to address it.

Matt's Journey
from DEFIER to DECIDER!

Matt views himself as a busy, productive guy. He's studying for his master's degree in communications, works part-time, and plays on a city soccer team. However, it soon became apparent to me that Matt was seldom as active as his schedule implied or warranted. If he was busy with anything, it was collecting slights, snubs and spending more energy refuting his obligations than meeting them.

Matt was becoming aware that his habit of dodging responsibilities was finally catching up with him. As a grad student, he had more independence to set his own deadlines as some assignments were open-ended. However, they were also more complex, particularly his independent field research. He recognized that this freedom could ultimately spell disaster. "I know it's self-sabotage," he confessed. "Still, whenever I feel pressured I have an overwhelming urge to do a disappearing act. I justify this by finding fault with the task. Old habits are hard to break."

Matt's prevailing work ethic had been to apply the minimum amount of effort needed to avoid being fired. He took pride in getting away with whatever he could; unconcerned about the below par reputation he had established for himself. His new job, however, was different. As a sales rep, he was essentially his own boss. He was working on commission: free to set his own hours, free to goof off. It was up to him whether he'd make any money. Now he was finding out the hard way that he had no idea about how to structure his time. After attending a motivational sales seminar provided by his company, Matt was hyped. He reported, "They gave us a pep talk about setting our own goals, then putting in the time and effort to meet them. I realize I've been so busy locking horns with others that I haven't had time to think about my own goals."

When I asked Matt about the origin of his defiance, he responded, "It began with my brother who was always the model student. He did whatever was expected of him. I viewed him as a guy with no spine, no mind of his own. I was a good student; I made my parents proud. But just to spite them, I always held back a bit. I refused to be a follower; I wouldn't mindlessly conform to what they wanted. I hated that my parents never saw me as an individual needing to find my own way in life. To them, I was a status symbol: their bright, athletic, handsome son who, of course, was supposed to succeed. I maintained this streak of rebellion to ensure that I was in control; that I had a life they couldn't touch."

Matt's conflict with his mom was intense. "I hated her nagging. It made me more resistant. I was sure I'd lose my identity if I caved in to her demands. I didn't want to be like my dad. He'd never align with me but would always back her up. He'd say stuff like: 'Do what your mother wants; listen to your mother; check with your mother first.' I couldn't stand that he never had the balls to disagree with her. So, I took on the job of doing it for both of us!"

When Matt enrolled in college, he was essentially free from daily parental control. That's when his procrastination truly kicked in. He'd skip classes just for the hell of it. He'd avoid reading assignments until an exam loomed. His papers were always thrown together at the last minute. "I harbored resentment toward most of my teachers," Matt recollected. "I felt that they didn't give a damn about me. Yet every now and then there was a professor like Dr. Brown, my art history instructor. Even though I didn't know anything about art, she was so enthusiastic about the subject and so interested in my perceptions that I wanted to do my best in her class."

Luckily, Matt's defiance didn't spread into all areas of his life. He attended soccer practices without fail, accepting and appreciating the coaching that was provided. Hence, he knew he was capable of modifying his habits. He just wasn't sure how to transfer this ability to his academic work.

Matt's First Steps Forward:

To kick off his change program, I helped Matt appreciate the difference between acting and reacting. *Acting,* I told him, is when *you're* in control. *You* choose to do what you want to do or need to do, not rebelliously but simply because that's your choice. *Reacting* is responding reflexively to what another person wants, either with compliance (like his brother) or defiance (like him). I'll tell you more about this in the Action Strategies section.

It took Matt quite some time to alter his knee-jerk defiance. But he didn't give up. He stayed with the change program, learning skills to tone down his rebellious nature, rev up his adventurous nature. You can learn them, too. Here's how.

Your Change Program
from DEFIANT to DETERMINED!

Creating new habits isn't easy but it also isn't as hard as you might imagine. Not if you do it step by step - even baby step by baby step. As you read this chapter, you'll learn many ways to help you curb your procrastination. However, I *don't* want you to do them all. Try and you'll become overwhelmed.

Hence, once you've finished this chapter, return to this page and scroll through the ideas I've gifted you. Then choose no more than *three skills you PROMISE yourself you'll implement NOW!* If you take on too much, you'll probably rebel silently or noisily (e.g. *"the hell with this!"*). So, be content with small changes that just might have a huge payoff!

This change program is designed to be *a reference* for you. So, once you've got a few skills under your belt, *return for more.* Just don't wait too long! Now, let's delve into specific strategies to guide you on your journey. Experiment with these strategies, taking care not to quit at the first sign of frustration. Be patient with your progress and be sure to notice when your defiance no longer controls what you do or don't do. Ready to begin your journey? Great! I'm psyched. Hope you are too!

THINKING To Get You Moving!

Know Where YOUR Power Lies.

Sorry to tell you this but the student role is *not* a power role. This means that you're not the one calling the shots. Others tell you what you're supposed to do, then grade you on your work. This is not an ideal position but remember you're in the student position *temporarily.* And you've chosen to be here to create a promising future for yourself. Hence, it's in your best interests to be as cooperative as you can reasonably be with rules, regulations and school authorities. This doesn't mean you need to be an automaton. You can certainly choose your courses as well as propose changes in procedures and assignments. Some professors and administrators may actually appreciate your input. But that won't happen unless you speak with them in a respectful manner.

When an assignment is given to you, does your mind race with reasons for why you shouldn't have to do it? Do you call the assignment 'unfair?' Do you envision ways to get out of it? If so, tone down your oppositional comeback. Then, generate alternative scenarios, like envisioning ways to do a project that satisfies your professor's requirements as well as your desires. This is what's termed a win-win solution! When you reflect on alternative ways to respond instead of automatically defying, you become empowered. So, rather than routinely rousing yourself into rebellion, think more temperately. Decide *how* you'll respond. Will you choose this course or that one? Choose this topic for your term paper or an alternative one? Recognize where your power lies instead of resisting power that's not yours.

Let's Get Going!

Let's suppose that your professor has given you a difficult field research project. Your initial response might be to:

- **Comply:** Say nothing; begin the project even though your heart isn't in it.
- **Defy:** Balk at doing it, allow your resentment to fester, your procrastination to flourish.
- **Defy Passive-Aggressively:** Agree to do it but neglect doing it.

Whichever option you choose, you probably won't do well, won't learn much and won't enjoy yourself. Imagine how much more fruitful your work could be if you applied constructive, creative thought to what you *could* do instead of being reflexively compliant or defiant. Here are two options to consider next time you're in this situation:

- **Imagine** alternative ways to approach a project that might make it more interesting, less intimidating. Then submit your ideas to your professor for approval. Chances are he'll be open to hearing you if he believes you're not just trying to get out of the work. When presenting your options, *be specific and positive* (e.g. for my child development paper, I'd like to work with an autistic child; would that be okay?). Veer away from being *global and negative* (e.g. I don't know any pre-school kids, so how do you expect me to do this project?). A bonus: You'll probably improve your relationship with your professor if you present your ideas in a well thought out, respectful manner.
- **Divide** the project into separate, smaller tasks. Then, figure out how to get each individual portion of the task accomplished most effectively. If you're feeling overwhelmed, shift competing projects to alternate time frames to make more time for this enterprise. No, you can't do it all - not at the same time anyway!

Choose Your Battles Carefully.

Reserve your acts of rebellion for important issues, weighing what's really worth fighting for. Maybe there's a situation in which you truly are being taken advantage of. Or a rule that's clearly discriminatory. Or an environmental issue that's offensive to your morality. For these types of situations, be a rebel!

I like **Margaret Mead's** words:

"Never doubt that a small group of thoughtful, committed citizens can change the world. Indeed, it's the only thing that ever has."

Avoid being *a rebel without a cause*. Though you may imagine yourself as a trailblazer, be sure you're not fooling yourself. Many defiers masquerade as rebels when their dissent is based on nothing deeper than - I don't want to do what I don't want to do!

Cultivate an Internal Nurturing Parent.

Our personalities are made up of diverse components with competing narratives. As a defier, I'm sure you're aware of your critical part – critical not only of others but also of yourself. But are you aware of your nurturing part? Not sure? Well then, pay close attention to the following exercise.

Let's Get Going!

Take a slow, deep breath. Take another one. Relax. Now imagine that inside you there lives a nurturing parent who is your very best friend. This parent is neither a critic nor a sidekick whom you use to support your own worst impulses. Rather, this nurturer is a mentor who speaks with maturity and compassion, helping you do what you need to do - even if you don't want to do it. Give your nurturing parent a name; either someone you admire or make up a name.

Now, picture a time when you're tempted to blow off your responsibilities, thinking why should *I* have to do this? Before you do anything, seek out the advice of your nurturing parent who will remind you of truths that you might otherwise overlook, such as:

- What you don't do now you may regret later on.
- Not everything you need to do has to feel good in the moment.
- What feels good in the short run may be a mistake in the long run.

Write down three more truths that your nurturing parent might remind you of. Then commit them to memory.

SPEAKING A New Narrative!

Limit Your Whining.

Health experts say that one or two glasses of wine a day are good for your health but more than that should be avoided. My take on it: One or two **whines** a day are good for your health but more than that should be avoided.

Yes, a little whining may actually improve your outlook on obligations. After all, life can be difficult. When things don't go your way, you've got to find some way to let off steam. "It's not fair! – "She shouldn't have said that!–" That's not right!" You complain, you grumble, you tell your story to a few empathetic friends and presto, you feel better. Astonishingly simple and effective therapy!

But whining that goes on day after day, well, that's a whine of another color. Chronic whiners typically perfect their art in childhood. Because nothing is as grating on the nerves as whining, some kids learn early on that it's a great way to manipulate parents. Mom and Dad give in to the most outrageous demands just to gain some peace and quiet. Like other childhood traits, however, whining is an activity that's best outgrown as you mature.

To be a winner, limit your whining. When you've reached your limit, you may be stymied about what to do if you're still feeling frustrated. Here are a few suggestions:

- When problems arise, search for solutions.
- When disappointments occur, distract yourself.
- When others annoy you, shrug it off.
- When situations need to be addressed, speak up.

Ignore these suggestions and whining may end up being your very best achievement! Surely, you don't want that to happen, do you?

Tone Down Confrontational Talk.

Minimize confrontational discourse, such as:

- "You gave me an unfair grade!"
- "You're always on my case!"
- "You expect too much from me!"

Notice that these negative gripes all begin with "you." Yes it's easy to let off steam this way but it doesn't help *resolve* any conflict. To attempt to resolve conflicts, best to begin your discourse with a respectful "I."

- "I believe I deserve a higher grade; can we discuss this matter?"
- "I'm sorry I missed my appointment; is this time good for you?"
- "I hope you noticed that I cleaned up my mess like you requested."

Hear the difference in tone? Are you aware that the "I" sentences are less blaming, less complaining, more open to exploring a solution?

"Maturity begins when we're content to feel we're right about something without feeling we need to prove someone else wrong."
~ Sydney Harris

Mean what You Say; Say what You Mean.

If you're asked to take care of a task, reflect on whether you'll do it in a timely manner *before* you say "yes." If you do commit, then realize you won't get it done on time, own up to it. Make sure you tell whoever was affected by your goof: (e.g. "I said I'd do the research but sorry I didn't get to it.") You can then propose a revised deadline such as, (e.g. "Could we meet tomorrow instead; I promise I'll complete it by then.")

What's *not* a good idea is to agree with others just to appease them. Then, take zero responsibility for blowing off what you agreed to do! This is classic passive-aggressive behavior that will not earn you any brownie points.

Apologize when it's Appropriate.

Some people hate making apologies. They equate an apology with an admission of failure or incompetence, like admitting that you're a screw-up or that you messed up and never do anything right! An apology, however, doesn't need to be anything so repugnant. It's simply a courtesy, a way to admit that what you did or didn't do negatively affected someone else. No need to go from one extreme (no apology) to the opposite extreme (self-flagellation). An apology can also be a prelude toward renegotiating what didn't work out, as in, "Sorry I didn't return your call yesterday. Do you have time to talk now?"

One more important point about apologies: Don't create a whole lot of situations where an apology is called for. Offering an apology without doing better next time is a classic passive-aggressive trait. You don't want to establish a reputation where your apologies are met with eye-rolling and a sarcastic "yeah, right!"

Let's Get Going!

Write down at least three apologies you might use next time one is called for. Make sure they're honest and appropriate. Don't denigrate yourself or you'll hesitate to use them. Here are my three favorites:

- "Sorry!" (simple but honest).
- "I apologize for being late with…."
- "I feel bad that I didn't take care of….. Can I make it up to you now?"

If you like my suggestions, own them, use them, put your own spin on them. Now, come up with *three more apologies of your own* that you'll feel comfortable using.

Reduce Your Negative Chatter.

Here are two descriptive sentences. Which one do you think is an easier trigger for procrastination?

- "It's a tough class with a ridiculous amount of required reading."
- "It's a tough class with a crazy amount of required reading but it's all interesting and I'm learning a lot."

The first sentence is so negative, why even bother to do the work? It seems like a waste of time. If you truly cannot find any redeeming value in the course, it may be best to withdraw.

The second sentence balances out the picture. Yes, you don't like all the required reading but you also remind yourself what you're learning. Remembering both the positive and negative aspects of a task helps motivate you to get going! Yes, some griping about an assignment is inevitable but please don't make that a habit. Gripe less, do more.

Be Aware of Your Non-Verbal Communication.

Have you ever had an argument that goes something like this?

- "What are **you** doing here?"
- "What do you mean what am **I** doing here? I have a right to be here; what's **your** problem?"
- "I just asked you what you're doing here."
- "Yeah, right!"

Many arguments are *not* about the words that are used. It's about the tone of voice, the body language, the facial expression, the non-verbal gestures. Linguistic studies reveal that at least 80% of communication is conveyed by those characteristics. Hence, if your words say *"yes, I'll do it"* but your non-verbals say *"no, quit bothering me,"* don't be surprised if others don't buy what you're selling.

ACTION Strategies!

Act rather than React.

Acting is when *you* choose to take action, not rebelliously but because you've made a choice about what you want or need to do.

Reacting is responding - often reflexively - to what someone else wants you to do. You could be compliant (do it) or defiant (don't do it). Either way *the other person* still defines the terms.

Acting is empowering. This is true whether you eventually get what you want or you don't. For example, if you believe it'll be difficult for you to complete a project by its due date, you may ask your professor for more time, explaining why. If the response is *"yes,"* you've gotten what you want - just be sure that you don't blow the new deadline. If the answer is a negotiated settlement, "yes, with a lowered grade" or "no, take an incomplete" you can then decide what to do. You're no worse off than you were initially.

When you advocate on your own behalf, you don't always get what you want, yet you can still feel pleased that you've acted in a manner that bolsters your personal power. To solidify this example, reflect on the difference between the roles of a powerful adult and a powerless child.

Adults - at least those who behave like adults - *act* by figuring out when and how to take care of their obligations.

Children - at least those who aren't 5 going on 50 - *react* by whining, wailing or throwing a tantrum when they don't get what they want. All unseemly behaviors, especially when you're no longer a kid.

Set up Reminders for Yourself.

Do what needs to be done. Don't wait till you fall behind, creating a need for a parental figure to berate you, punish you or nag you about your obligations. If you need a reminder about your obligations, apps will kindly remind you what you need to do. If you're the non-tech type, Post-it notes, calendar reminders, even scribbled notes on your desk can work. Which do you believe is a winning strategy - figuring out a way to remind yourself of your obligations or waiting until an authority figure berates you for what you didn't do?

Work with Your Team, not against Your Team.

As independent as you'd like to imagine you are, you're still dependent upon others for many things. You may be dependent on your parents for your college expenses, your friends for your emotional well-being, your professors for your academic success. This doesn't make you a weak person; it's just a dose of reality.

So, whether you're at home with your parents, on campus with your friends or in class with your fellow students, things go smoother when you function as a *team player*, not as a rebel bucking the system. Hence, get into the habit of supporting and aiding others. Give up the habit of withholding and obstructing. Be open to accommodating what the team expects from you as well as what you expect from the team.

Pursue Activities Where You're in Control.

Not everything needs to be a team effort. If you have a strong need to do things *your way*, express that need with creative, constructive projects you can completely control. It might be a:

- Creative activity: write a song, create a painting
- Athletic activity: run a marathon, pump up your body
- Organizational activity: formulate your files, rearrange your room

Be innovative, not defiant. When you're in control of *some* aspects of your life, you'll have less need to control *all* aspects of your life.

Be Assertive rather than Aggressive.

It may seem counterproductive for you to become more assertive if you're already a defier; isn't that for passive people who can't speak up for themselves? Yes and no. When I taught assertiveness training, most of my students were passive people who needed to gain the skills, strategies and confidence to become more assertive. A few students, however, were *aggressive* people who needed to learn how to sandpaper down their rough edges. Though these students thought they were being assertive, they discovered that others experienced them as aggressive, abrasive and even abusive.

Assertiveness training teaches you to become more empowered, not by defying but by:

- Initiating ideas
- Communicating concerns
- Clarifying misunderstandings
- Forging compromises
- Proposing changes
- Motivating others – and more

Becoming proficient in the above skills will take you far, not just in academia but in advancing your career and forging friendships.

Let's Get Going!

Imagine that you're the lucky recipient of a gift certificate to an assertiveness training course. Although your initial thought is to toss the certificate in the trash, you give it a second thought. Now that your defiance is no longer in full gear, write down *three skills* you'd like to learn in the course that would be valuable to you. Examples of these might be:

- How to communicate effectively with authority figures
- How to deal with disappointment
- How to quell your negativity

Once you've decided on the skills, go to your favorite search engine. Read what they say about the skills you've chosen. Open up a new document; write down at least three important ideas you've learned. Vow to put your new learning into practice.

GUIDED IMAGERY
Relax and Let Go!

What do you imagine your life would be like if you used your energy to *achieve your goals* rather than to resist the status quo? Not sure? Perhaps the following guided imagery will offer you a few cues.

Choose a comfortable place to sit that's quiet, dimly lit and free from distractions. Take a few deep breaths to relax your body, s-l-o-w-l-y inhaling through your nose, then s-l-o-w-l-y exhaling through your mouth. Let go of any tension or tightness in your body. Allow the thoughts and cares of the day to drift away, leaving your body light, your mind empty.

Read each section of the visualization slowly, pausing for about 20 seconds between each instruction. Or, have someone else read it to you so you can close your eyes, relax and let your mind just be. Let's begin!

Picture yourself when you were a little kid, engaged in a fun activity with friends. Maybe you're playing ball, running around, singing, painting or just having a good time. *Imagine the freedom you felt then.* Imagine the expression on your face when you were enjoying yourself.

Now picture yourself a few years older. You're still running around having fun but *now you're involved in team sports.* You want to do your best to help your team. You feel a bit of pressure but it still feels good to be on the team, enjoying yourself and striving to do your best.

Return to your present age. *Picture yourself engaged in a pursuit today that brings you similar sentiments.* Envision the enjoyment you experience when you engage in an activity without resentment or resistance.

Now bring to mind a task in your present life that you don't want to do but that you realize *needs to be done.* Imagine - even if it's not true - that you're choosing to do this task with your own free will. Then go about doing it in the same relaxed, pleasurable way that you went about doing the previous activity.

Picture finishing this task, feeling delighted that it's finally done. Take pride in the fact that you worked on it without resistance or rebellion. Hear a voice inside you saying, "You can enjoy doing a task even if it's not of your own choosing. When it's finally finished, you'll feel energized and empowered!" Pause for a moment to realize the truth in these words.

Take time to absorb the meaning of your visualization before you move on to the next section. Write down what you want to remember. If you wish, record the instructions so you can play them back at a later date to see what new imagery may come to mind.

What's Your Next Step?

Congratulations! You've completed the program for defiers. Now take a moment to simply relax and breathe deeply. I hope you don't feel overwhelmed by all the valuable information in this chapter. Yes, you can read it all but you can't absorb it all - at least not right away.

So, go back and scroll through the change program. Choose no more than *three skills you PROMISE yourself you'll implement NOW!* Learning these skills is a prerequisite for outsmarting your procrastination. But it's not just learning them; it's putting them into practice and retaining them. You'll do that, right?

I hope you remember what I said at the beginning of the change program. It's designed to be *a reference* for you. Take in what you can use now. Then when you're ready, return to the program to see what's next for you. Just don't wait too long!

Never forget that your personality style has many great qualities. You're not afraid to question authority. You're self-reliant. You're brave. You're bold. Excellent! Now you've got to use those traits to advance your education rather than allowing them to stop you from being all you can be!

Now might be a good time for a short break. Get up and stretch. Do a few squats. Grab your favorite snack. I wouldn't mind if you share some with me; my stomach's growling! Then move on to the next chapter to continue your journey. There's a lot more to learn.

"Until you make peace with who you are,
you'll never be content with what you have."
~ **Doris Mortman**

CHAPTER 9

THE PLEASER
...BUT I CAN'T SAY "NO!"

Welcome Pleasers! You have many fine qualities. You're good-natured, gracious and agreeable. You enjoy doing for others. Sounds like great qualities for a fine human being and a first-rate resume for Miss Congeniality or Mr. Nice Guy. So what could be wrong?

Too often *your* needs end up at the bottom of the pile. Frazzled and frenzied by not enough time to do it all, you need to *chill out* before you *burn out*. In this chapter, you'll gain a deeper understanding of your pleaser personality and how it can create trouble for you.

What are some of the telltale signs of a pleaser procrastinator? Here's a mini-version of the quiz you took earlier. See if these questions resonate with you.

- Do I have difficulty saying "no" to others?
- Do I find it hard to set priorities for myself?
- Do I run around doing a lot yet don't always get to what I really want or need to do?

Our speedy, success-oriented culture puts pressure on all of us to work faster, harder, better. This is a troublesome situation for many but it's particularly tough for pleasers as you're already inclined to take on too much. Though some may perceive you as a 'do-aholic,' the dizzying array of activities you're involved in may not be because you can't stop doing but because it's tough for you to say *"no"* to others. With too much on your plate, something's gotta give!

Though media stories may try to convince you that you can have it all, you can't! Attempt to do too much and you'll be operating on overload. To truly understand what that means, let's examine what occurs when an electrical circuit is on overload.

You're working hard one evening trying to finish a report. All of a sudden, you're in total darkness. The circuit breaker has popped. No lights, no charger, no printer, no microwave, no toaster, no A/C, no TV, no nothing. What do you do? You search for the popped breaker on the electrical panel. You flip the breaker back on and return to doing your stuff. You've just settled in when pop, you're in total darkness again. You realize that you forgot to turn off an apparatus or two before you returned to work. Frustrated, you think, what a pain in the neck this circuit breaker is.

Then you remember what it's designed to do. It's a *safety device* protecting you from fire that would undoubtedly occur if you continued to operate on overload. Suddenly it becomes obvious to you that *you* also need to have a safety device. Your harried, pressured, stressed life means *you're* operating on overload.

If you didn't have so much to do, you wouldn't be so stressed about your upcoming exam. If you weren't so stressed about your exam, you wouldn't be so nervous about the paper you've got to write. If you weren't so nervous about the paper you need to write, you wouldn't be so upset about your roommate's reprimand. If you weren't so upset about your roommate's reprimand, you wouldn't have this pounding headache! Get the picture?

Too bad you don't have circuit breakers built into your system to alert you of an impending overload. Or, do you? Imagine that:

- **Chronic stress** is a way your *body* is telling you: "Stop! You're damaging me. Treat me better or I won't function well!"
- **Chronic worrying** is a way your *mind* is telling you: "Stop! You can't continue to live this way. Give me a break!"
- **Chronic conflict** is a way your *relationships* are telling you: "Stop! You're trying too hard to please everybody. Just be yourself!"

Warning signals, like circuit breakers, are designed to protect you from harm. If you neglect to ease up on the pressure you put on yourself, you can do serious damage to your mind, body and relationships. I hope you're wise enough not to let that happen.

Two Pleaser Styles

Now it's time for me to introduce you to two pleasers who are pleasing everyone - except themselves.

Social Butterfly Pleaser

Brianna admits to being an approval junkie, judging her worth on how popular she is. Since her social life takes precedence, it's no surprise that her academic life suffers. Though Brianna doesn't view herself as a procrastinator, she does acknowledge that there never seems to be enough time in the day for her to do all that's expected of her.

"When I'm by myself," Brianna laments, "I feel empty. I hate being alone for any length of time. I start to study but am easily seduced into checking in with friends on social media. Then I get hooked, finding it hard to get off." Brianna keeps so busy hanging with friends, responding to a barrage of text messages and posting on social media that her academic assignments end up at the bottom of the pile. "Studying is lonely work," she says. "I like spending time with friends. Then before I know it, the day's gone."

Overly Responsible Pleaser

Brandon is not nearly as sociable as Brianna, but he's also a pleaser. Instead of currying favor with others to please them, he seeks to impress others with all that he does. Hence, like Brianna, he's overworked and underprepared to meet his academic obligations. Brandon's pattern of taking on responsibility began early in life. "I've always been the strong one in my family," he told me. "My dad died when I was 12. Instantly, I became 'the man of the house.' I started working at 15 to bring in extra money for the family. That's when I developed a habit of being busy all the time. It seemed to be the responsible thing to do. I know something's not right, however, because I'm always feeling hassled."

Brandon is a varsity member of the track team, active in student organizations and carries a heavy course load. He also assumes more than his fair share of household work. "My roommate's a slob," he griped, "so I'm the one who cleans up, fixes things, and deals with problems in the apartment. If I complain to him, he shrugs it off." It seems as if Brandon's roommate is imposing an unfair burden on him, yet he admits that he actually doesn't mind being the one in charge. With pride he said, "I don't have close friends but I do have lots of people who count on me. The problem is that with all I do for others, I barely have enough time to do my own work."

Four Pleaser Traits

Overloaded with Obligations

Pleasers believe that their value is based on how others view them. Hence, they keep trying to prove their worthiness by doing for others. Saying "no," they see as a sign of selfishness. Asking for help, they see as a sign of weakness. So it's no surprise when pleasers end up with an overload of obligations, which then becomes the root of their procrastination.

Both Brianna and Brandon reflexively say "yes" to others, whether they have the time, energy or desire to make another commitment. This diversion of energy takes its toll on their educational goals. Brianna, the social butterfly, finds it tough to make time for her school work, while Brandon's excess of responsibilities leaves measly time for his academic responsibilities.

> *"What we must decide is HOW we are valuable -*
> *rather than how valuable we are."*
> ~ Edgar Friedenberg

Reflexively Say "Yes"

Instead of actively deciding for themselves *what* they're going to do, as well as *when* and *how* they'll do it, pleasers reflexively say *"yes"* to whatever or whoever is calling for them in the moment. With so many activities and people competing for their attention, it's tough to put academic responsibilities front and center. Pleasers need to learn to make conscious decisions about what they'll say "yes" to; otherwise their academic obligations will continue to get the short end of the stick.

Brianna stays heavily involved with her friends to the detriment of her schoolwork. And Brandon spreads himself too thin with too many activities. Though he likes being busy on all fronts, the quality of his work suffers because of the time he spends on other obligations. Like Brianna, he confuses *"more"* with *"better."*

Academic Work takes Low Priority

When you're in college, academic responsibilities need to come first. All the time? No, definitely not. But if your social life frequently takes precedence over your academic responsibilities, you're asking for trouble! Creating a workable balance between academia and everything else that's vying for your attention isn't easy, yet it's essential.

Since Brianna's social life takes precedence over her studies, it's no surprise that her academic life suffers. And though Brandon isn't nearly as sociable as Brianna, his extracurricular activities make it tough for him to spend sufficient time on school work.

Difficulty Creating a Well-Balanced Life

Pleasers are most familiar with two polarized states of being - being overly busy or being completely wiped out. Often pleasers say they wish they could just relax but when the opportunity arises, they're somehow at a loss. As their self-importance is based on being busy, it's not easy for them to create a slower, less hassled life.

Brianna doesn't enjoy whatever downtime she has. She feels buggy being alone and is forever yearning to be with others. When Brandon has nothing to do, he feels barren, admitting "I grew up too fast; I wish I could be a kid again without a care in the world."

Hannah's Journey
from EXTERNAL to INTERNAL!

Hannah had no trouble admitting that academic work has not been her top priority. "I work part-time, sing in the chorus, take part in drama club productions and am involved in student government. I thought I was doing so well but now I see I'm overextended. I fooled myself into thinking I was some sort of super achiever and could do it all!"

Hannah could no longer avoid facing the truth about herself; she wasn't going to graduate with her friends. What a disappointment! Some of her friends were already beginning their careers. "I can't wait to graduate; then land a fulltime job in sports marketing!" she exclaimed at our first meeting. "I want to prove to myself that I can have an exciting, successful career."

As we discussed Hannah's history, she revealed that she came from a family of procrastinators. "Both my parents talk a lot about what they're going to do. They sound so sincere but I've learned that their ideas are flights of fancy. My mother's always dropping her own projects to help others; then complains that she has no time for herself. And my father's too tired by the weekend to do the things he promised he'd do." Speaking about her dad, Hannah recalled, "When I was a kid, there were many times he'd promise to take me somewhere special. Then at the last minute he'd weasel out with some excuse."

Her disappointment over her father's reneging fueled her own insistence on not disappointing others. Reflecting back, however, she could see how often she reneged on her promises to herself - akin to what her dad did to her when she was younger. Doing whatever the crowd was doing, fitting in, pleasing her friends, these are what took precedence over her own desires. Hannah was particularly embarrassed about her behavior with her high school boyfriend. "Whatever I thought would please him, I'd do. I even went to his house to clean his room. My friends thought I was crazy but I figured what's the big deal? I like to organize things, so I'll organize his stuff. I knew he needed it. I didn't see then that I was hurting myself by doing so much for him."

As Hannah and I worked together, she became increasingly introspective. The first time I asked her, *"What do you want to do about a specific situation,"* she was stymied by the question. She knew what *she should* do, what *others wanted* her to do, but she had never thought about what *she* wanted to do. Clearly, it was time for Hannah to focus on her own wants and needs.

> *"Your vision will become clear when you look into your heart.*
> *Who looks outside, dreams. Who looks inside, awakens."*
> **Carl Jung**

Hannah's First Steps Forward:

Hannah's first objective was to give priority to her own goals. If she could do that, then she wouldn't be so susceptible to pleasing others or to tending to random events of the day. Together, we worked on a program to help her create daily priorities.

Her most successful strategy was to deliberately question up front whether a project was her own agenda or someone else's. Her goal was not to reject someone else's but to make sure she made room for her own. To keep herself on track, she learned how to say *"no"* to others in a gracious manner. *"No, but thanks for asking me"* became part of her lingo. Over time, Hannah developed additional skills to create a workable balance between meeting her own needs and the needs of others. You can learn them too. Here's how.

Your Change Program
from CONSENT to CONSIDER!

Creating new habits isn't easy but it also isn't as hard as you might imagine. Not if you do it step by step - even baby step by baby step. As you read this chapter, you'll learn many ways to curb your procrastination. However, I *don't* want you to do them all. Try and you'll become overwhelmed guaranteed!

Hence, once you've finished reading this chapter, return to this page and scroll through the ideas I've given you. Then choose no more than *three skills that you PROMISE yourself you'll implement NOW!* As you put these skills into practice, you'll feel less hassled by the need to please.

I've designed this change program to be *a reference* for you. So once you've got a few skills under your belt, *return for more.* Just don't wait too long! And be sure to compliment yourself when you notice that you're paying more attention to what *you* need and want to do. Now, let's delve into specific strategies to help you curb your tendency to procrastinate. Ready to begin your journey? Great! I'm psyched. Hope you are too!

THINKING To Get You Moving!

Choose Your Priorities.

Say goodbye to the Superman/Superwoman myth. Quit aiming for having it all: top grades, athletic achievements, extra-curricular activities, popularity superstar, foreign travel, prized internship, hot love life, fab friends, close family connections. Instead, pay more attention to what *you* need to do to achieve your immediate goals.

Since you can't have it all (really you can't), make day-by-day choices about how you'll use your time and energy. If you find yourself neglecting any aspect of your life for too long, adjust your priorities. Not only can't you have it all, you also can't *do* it all. Not all by yourself anyway. So, experiment with working in groups. Request assistance from others. Seek input from professors. Involve others in projects, so you don't need to do everything by yourself. As a pleaser, you're there for others. Let them be there for you too.

Seek Approval from Yourself.

Make decisions about how you're going to spend your day. How much time will you spend on school work? How much time will you spend on social life and extra-curricular activities? If you get seduced into chasing pursuits simply to fit in or to gain approval from others, nip this attitude in the bud. Learn to live by the rules that make sense to you, not by the dictates of others. Then, pat yourself on the back when you notice you're raising your grades and feeling good about yourself!

Though it may temporarily feel good to win a friend's favor, make sure it's *not essential* to your well-being. If you do decide to accommodate others, insist that it fits into your time schedule. Nix the guilt if you don't do what a friend wants. Nix the fear of offending others. You have a right to pick and choose how you'll spend your time. In no way am I suggesting that you become egotistical or self-centered. Being a generous, giving person is an admirable quality. Accommodating others just to win their approval or prove your popularity is another matter.

Balance Your Obligations.

- Time for *work*, time for *play*.
- Do what *you* want, do what *others* want.
- Stuff to do *today*; stuff to do *tomorrow*.

It's all a balancing act. And it's tough to walk a fine line between doing it all. So what do you do? Read on!

Let's Get Going!

Open a new document and *write down* the answer to these questions:

- What do I spend *too much time* doing?
- What do I spend *insufficient time* doing?
- How will I balance what I *want* to do with what I *need* to do?
- How will I balance what I *do for others* with what I *do for myself*?
- What steps will I take that'll help me make more conscious decisions?

Once you take the time to reflect on these questions, you'll know what you need to do to create a better balance for yourself. The ideal situation is when what *you want* to do, what you *need* to do and what *others* want you to do are one and the same. But the ideal situation doesn't often occur. Hence, the trick is to learn to walk a fine line between all of your needs and wants, which invariably means saying "no" to some things.

Dump Your Helpless Mentality.

Day-to-day pressures will feel overwhelming if you believe that you've no choice in what you do or how you do it. Or, that what you're doing is not enough - unless you add *one more* activity to your day. Shy away from a victim, "poor-me" mindset. Instead, start viewing yourself as the one who is in charge of your life. Do this by recognizing that *you* are the one who *decides* what courses to take, *creates* structure to your day, *balances* your priorities, *manages* your time and *maintains* your relationships. True, you need to work within the contingencies of a situation. But simply because you're not in control of everything, doesn't mean you're not in control of anything.

"People often say that a person has not yet found himself.
But the self is not something one finds,
it's something one creates."
~ Thomas Szasz

SPEAKING A New Narrative!

Learn How to say "NO!"

Saying "no" when you're thinking "no" can reap unexpected benefits, such as:

- You'll be in charge of your day.
- You'll build character - character is weakened by simply following the crowd.
- Your "yes" will be respected - people take for granted those who say "yes" to everything.

Your "no" can be:
- **Polite:** "No, I can't join you but thanks for asking."
- **Accommodating:** "No, today isn't good for me; maybe tomorrow."
- **Direct:** "No I'm not going."
- **Harsh:** "Didn't you hear me? I told you I'm NOT going!"

You'll probably use the harsh type of *"no"* sparingly, saving it for those who consistently brush off what you've said. Grant yourself the freedom to use whatever type of *"no"* best fits your situation and mood.

Let's Get Going!

Change favors the prepared mind. So, let's get prepared. Open up a document. Recall a situation in which you know you'd have been better off saying "no," but somehow got sucked into saying "yes." If you were in that same situation today, how would you handle it? Think of the exact words you'd use. Write down those words. Look at them every once in a while. I guarantee you a similar situation will occur and this time you'll be prepared!

End Sentences on an Upbeat Note.

When you're feeling overwhelmed with your obligations, you may say things that trigger a feeling that it's all too much:

- "I'm swamped with work."
- "This pace is killing me."
- "I have no idea where to begin."

Even if these statements are true, you can still end your sentence on an upbeat note by using one of our friendly three-letter words.

- "I'm swamped with work *and* I'm glad I got some of it done today."
- "This pace is killing me *but* thankfully spring break is almost here."
- "I don't know where to begin *but* I can begin writing an outline."

Do you see how you can make your *but* work *for you* rather than using it as an excuse for not doing your stuff? Do you hear how the heart and soul of your communication changes when you end your sentence on an upbeat note? Speak about yourself as a person who can deal well with difficult situations, then rejoice when you notice you're turning into just that kind of person!

> *"Thinking too well of people often allows them*
> *to be better than they otherwise would."*
> ~ Nelson Mandela

Use Empowering Words.

Let your language reflect your strength. Replace weak phrases such as:

- *I'm supposed to...*
- *I'm expected to...*
- *She wants me to...*
- *He needs me to...*

with strong phrases such as:

- *I've decided to...*
- *I'm determined to...*
- *I've chosen to...*
- *I've made a commitment to...*

As you begin to take responsibility for your choices, you won't be so driven by the need to please. When you're not so driven by the need to please, your confidence will rise - along with your grades!

Speak Enthusiastically about Downtime.

If you follow the cultural command to do, do, do, your life can easily spin out of control. So rather than waiting till you're overwhelmed, give yourself downtime.

It could be for an hour, a day, a weekend, a week. It's okay if you're not forever busy. If you hear yourself saying, "I got nothing done the whole weekend," stop. No need to scold yourself. You're entitled to downtime. Indeed, it'd be great if you could make a habit of saying positive statements about downtimes such as, "It feels great having a weekend off!"

Take a moment to think of two more positive statements about down-time. Instead of skipping over it, do it! Your life will be more carefree and comfortable when you give yourself "off" times instead of setting up a schedule for yourself in which you're "on" all the time.

ACTION Strategies!

Be More Proactive, Less Reactive.

- **Proactive:** when you *seize the initiative before* trouble happens.
- **Reactive:** when you *respond* to a situation *after* trouble has happened.

As a student, you're unable to seize the initiative about most of your assignments. Just the fact that they are assignments (assigned *to* you) indicates that you're not in charge. However, you can still be proactive with some of your assigned tasks. How? At times the answer is easy.

I taught Intro Psych courses for several years. I believe that the more interested you are in a topic, the more you'll learn. Hence, I gave my students lots of leeway for choosing a topic for their term paper. My instructions were simple: Using at least 3 resources, write a 1500-word paper on **any topic** relating to human behavior that stirs your interest. Imagine that you're the professor and I'm the student. Make sure I learn something that will engage my attention when I read your paper.

Quite naively, I thought my students would be delighted with such an open-ended assignment. A few were. But for many, it stirred up their 'pleasing' anxiety:

- But what do *you want* me to do?
- But how do *you want* me to approach the subject?
- But what type of resources do *you want* me to use?
- But how will *you grade* me?

Clearly, I had not offered the pleasers in my class enough structure. They plaintively cried out, "tell me what to do!" Even if your professor is not encouraging you to be proactive, you can still maintain a proactive attitude. Josh understood that when he proudly proclaimed, "I thought I'd hate statistics but I learned a lot about calculating the odds. Spring break, I'm off to Vegas. I can't wait for this course to have a payoff at the craps table." So, even if the course is designed for one purpose, nothing prevents you from using your new knowledge for your own purposes.

Let's Get Going!

Despite your need to focus on academic requirements, some of the most valuable experiences of college life are those that are gained *outside* the classroom. I'll mention three: forging new friendships, engaging in cultural events, participating in sports activities. Okay, now it's your turn. Write down three more experiences that you believe will enrich your life. Why am I emphasizing this point? Since you're a pleaser, I want to make sure that one of the people you please is *you*. I want you to be excited and energized by an aspect of college life that's particularly meaningful to you. I hope you want that for yourself as well.

> *"It's not enough to have a good mind.*
> *The main thing is to use it well."*
> ~ **Rene Descartes**

Eliminate, Delegate, Consolidate.

I'm sure you've noticed that some people are more efficient with their use of time than others. It's like they have 28 hours in the day instead of your measly 24. How do they do it? One way I've already mentioned is to say "no" to some activities so that you have time for others without becoming overwhelmed. Here are three other ways to use your time efficiently.

Eliminate:
Yes, you can eliminate social media during finals week. So what if others are posting and tweeting. You know your priorities. You know what's important to you. You know that you don't have to do what everyone else is doing just to fit in.

Delegate:
Delegate and/or share the work. Sometimes it's school work; sometimes it's maintenance work. As a pleaser, you may be the one that others have been delegating responsibilities to. Now it's time to even up the score. If you're unsure about what to say, review the speaking section - especially the part where I tell you *"know how to say "no."*

Consolidate:
You'll be a lot more efficient when you consolidate several actions into one. A little planning ahead means you combine two shopping trips into one, two library trips into one. Put time into planning ahead and you'll end up with more time for yourself.

Ask for Help when You Need it.

Pleasers are accustomed to being the helper, not the helpee. Nothing wrong with helping, just make sure you have a fair balance between what you give and what you get.

If you need clarification about an assignment, ask your professor, TA or fellow students. You're certainly not the only one who can't figure out what your professor meant or how detailed she wants the report to be. We all need a helping hand from time to time. Others will not think less of you when you ask for assistance. Indeed, it's just as likely to make them think more highly of you for *valuing* their assistance. But if anyone does respond in a brusque manner, remember he has a right to say "no" too. Too bad he never learned to say it graciously.

Weigh the Pros and Cons of New Opportunities.

Let's suppose you've been offered an opportunity to create a podcast describing an innovative research project you've been involved in. You'd love to take advantage of the opportunity but you also worry that you might be overextending yourself. What to do?

First, steer clear of reflexively saying "yes," then reacting to this opportunity as one more obligation to take care of, sigh! Instead, focus on whether you have the time, energy and desire to take advantage of it. Do this by:

- **Asking** how much time the project will take
- **Making** a pro-con list for yourself
- **Negotiating** with the powers to be about the work involved
- **Sharing** the responsibility with another student
- **Creating** a later start date when you'll have more time

Get the idea? Your answer need not be an automatic "yes" or "no." You want to think it through to see if you have the time, energy and interest before you decide what you'll do.

Join Study Groups.

Most college assignments are expected to be done on a solo basis. This is not always the best way to learn. Nor does it model many work environments. At work, colleagues are typically supportive of one another. They brainstorm to develop creative ideas. They appreciate the importance and excitement of working with a team to create a finished project.

If your professors neglect the group process, viewing all learning as individual achievements, be proactive. Create a study group on your own. Or, an exploratory group that builds community and gets answers to questions.

Discuss ideas, review chapters, answer each other's questions and offer honest feedback. Give and get!

GUIDED IMAGERY
Relax and Let Go!

Instead of focusing on pleasing others, how about cultivating a frame of mind that's focused on what *you* need and want to do? The following guided imagery will steer you in that direction.

Choose a comfortable place to sit that's quiet, dimly lit and free from distractions. Take a few deep breaths to relax your body, s-l-o-w-l-y inhaling through your nose, then s-l-o-w-l-y exhaling through your mouth. Let go of any tension or tightness in your body. Allow the thoughts and cares of the day to drift away, leaving your body light, your mind empty.

Read each section of the visualization slowly, pausing for about 20 seconds between each instruction. Or, have someone else read it to you so you can close your eyes, relax and let your mind just be. Let's begin!

Picture yourself strolling along a path in a densely wooded area. You don't know where you are but you're content to keep on walking. When you go deeper into the woods, you reach a V-shaped fork where the path splits into two. Both paths look the same, so you're not sure which one to take. *You believe your friend would take the path to the right* so you start down that one, even though you're feeling doubtful about whether it's the best one for you.

As you continue to walk down the path, you notice that the trees are now closer together. You're becoming a bit nervous. Still, you keep walking till you arrive at another crossroads: one path on your left, one on your right and a third straight ahead. All three paths look the same so once more you don't know which one to take. *You wonder which path your parents would want you to take.* You're still unsure but you don't want to waste any more time so you proceed down the one to the left.

As you keep on walking, you turn a bend. All of a sudden the path ends. You turn around; *the path behind you has disappeared.* Oh my God! You're lost among all these trees. You're scared. You're shocked. You're terrified!

You tell yourself, *"don't panic; stop and think!"* You try to stay calm. You lean against a tree, take a few deep breaths and look high up into the woods. Suddenly, you notice a tower that's not too far away. You decide to walk toward it. As you walk, you realize the tower's even closer than you thought. In just a few minutes, it's in front of you!

The tower has many steps leading to the top. Though the stairs don't look as sturdy as you'd like *you decide to climb them – slowly and carefully.*

You're now at the peak of the tower, out of breath and exhausted. Still, you feel elated that you can clearly see over the surrounding treetops. Looking ahead, you notice a stream with a path running along its bank, ending at an inn with a *"Welcome"* sign out front. *You feel relieved, knowing there's a path for you to follow.*

You carefully climb down the tower and walk through the woods toward the inn. When you arrive you enter the inn, aware of how inviting it feels. You see a comfortable, cozy chair waiting for you in the front room. You sink down into it, heave a sigh of relief and relax. You close your eyes and hear a self-assured voice saying, *"Rise above where you are to take a good look at where you want to go. Then follow your path!"*

Take comfort in the words you've just heard. Notice how calm you feel. Be aware of the message of this exercise. Have you taken a good look at where you want to go? Are you ready to go there, without getting waylaid by so many distractions? Write down what you want to remember from your imagery. If you wish, record the instructions so you can play them back at a later date to see what new imagery may come to mind.

What's Your Next Step?

Congratulations! You've completed the program for pleasers. Now take a moment to simply relax and breathe deeply. I hope you don't feel overwhelmed by all the valuable information in this chapter. Yes, you can read it all but you can't absorb it all - at least not right away.

So, go back and scroll through the change program and choose no more than *three skills that you PROMISE yourself you'll implement NOW!* Learning these skills is a prerequisite for outsmarting your procrastination. But it's not just learning them; it's putting them into practice and retaining them. You'll do that, right?

I hope you remember what I said at the beginning of the change program. It's designed to *be a reference* for you. Take in what you can use now. Then when you're ready, return to the program to see what's next for you. Just don't wait too long!

Never forget that your personality style has many great qualities. You're good-natured, agreeable and enjoy doing for others. Excellent! Just don't let your pleasing qualities stop you from being all you can be.

Now might be a good time to take a short break. Get up and stretch. Do a few of your favorite exercises. Grab a snack. If it's ice cream, you don't need to be told who's coming over to share some with you! Then move on to the very last chapter that's packed with information for all six styles of procrastination.

"The worst loneliness is not to be comfortable with yourself."
~ Mark Twain

CHAPTER 10

LET'S WRAP IT UP!

You've almost finished the book. I hope your mind has been stretched. I hope you have exciting ideas whirring around in your gray cells. I hope you're fired up about all that you've learned. I'm a hopeful person. Can you tell?

> *"One's mind, once stretched by a new idea,*
> *never regains its original dimension."*
> **Oliver Wendell Holmes**

Now that you've learned the skills to outsmart your procrastination, all is good, right? Maybe, maybe not! I've pointed you in the right direction. I've given you ideas to get you going but I can't *make* you give up your procrastination. I can, however, share with you some sticky wickets that might derail your progress. Forewarned is forearmed.

On Track, Off Track

There'll be days when you're on track – you're inspired, you're motivated; you're proud of yourself. Yay! Then there are other days when you fall into a rut. You seem to have forgotten all you've learned. Bummer!

What happened? Sorry to say it's the norm, not the exception, to lapse into old self-defeating patterns. It may be a specific hurdle that's throwing you off course or a general downturn in your life. No matter the cause. The solution is to view your setback as temporary and *get back on track as soon as possible*. Here are four ways to help you do that:

Believe in yourself

Never doubt your ability to emerge from your rut. Nix the shame; shame undercuts your worth. Nix the guilt; guilt makes it harder to bounce back. Talk to a nurturing person. Watch an upbeat movie. Listen to music you love. Feel your positive energy returning. Then get going!

Keep your mind active

Everyone knows that exercising is the tried and true road to a buff body. But do you know that exercising your brain is the tried and true road to a first-class mind? So, reflect on an exciting idea you've learned. Get keyed up about it. Focus on the possibilities. Then notice your energy rising, your motivation returning!

Keep your hero by your side

Your hero can be real or mythical, male or female, alive or dead. You and your hero are a team that can't be beat. Envision your hero saying encouraging things to you; pumping you up when you're feeling down. Your hero is giving you the strength you need to get back On Track!

Recall when you were On Track

Remember how good you felt! How much energy you had! Look, there's a bridge in front of you that goes from Off Track to On Track. You and your hero hop on it. You start walking. You keep walking, singing a song as you move along. Now you're jogging. Now you're running. Now you're just about there! Yes, you're back On Track where you belong.

Regrets: Coulda, Woulda, Shoulda

Regrets serve a worthwhile purpose - *if* you learn from them. If you regret that you didn't outline your paper *before* you started writing it, outline your paper the next time around. This may seem like an obvious strategy, yet for many it's not. Rigidity may keep you stuck doing things the same way – even when that way isn't working for you.

So, reflect on what you did wrong. Then, decide on a course of action that'll keep new regrets at bay. For example, if you're thinking of skipping class, hopefully for a good reason, contact a classmate in advance who'd be willing to share notes and discuss class content with you. Much better than getting upset after the fact and saying, "Why didn't I think of it before?"

Guilt: Healthy or Neurotic

Healthy guilt serves a purpose by prodding you into doing what you know you need to do. If you've scheduled a study session one evening and there's a party happening down the hall, healthy guilt keeps your nose to the grindstone. Smart thinking! You're looking out for yourself by refusing to be seduced by everyday distractions.

Neurotic guilt, in contrast, is like the Energizer Bunny; it keeps going and going. No matter what you did right, there's always something you did wrong. Wallowing in guilt, like nursing regrets, robs you of your positive energy, decreasing your ability to focus and do.

Criticism: Helpful and Hurtful

You may believe there's nothing about you to be criticized. Whatever you think is amazing; whatever you say is awesome; whatever you do is astonishing! Sorry, it's not true. Here's what **Winston Churchill** said about criticism:

"Criticism may not be agreeable, but it is necessary."

Though it's easier to accept criticism when it's offered constructively, it's still a good idea to listen to it regardless of how it's presented. Most academic criticism will focus on what's *wrong* with your work, not what's right with it. Some may even be harsh and demeaning. Instead of blowing off the criticism or letting it paralyze you, take a deep breath. Remind yourself of all your good qualities. Then, review the criticism to see what value it may have for you.

Digital Technology: Helpful or Harmful?

Digital technology can be your best friend or your worst enemy. It can help you get things done or it can suck up your time. Though the hypnotic allure of the Web will always be there, the Web itself may help you resist it. How can it do that? Let me show thee the ways.

Block distractions

The time you spend playing games, posting on social media and aimless surfing can rob you of the time you need to achieve your goals. But how do you stop yourself from doing these activities when you're so drawn to them?

You can do the obvious: close your email; shut down your social media sites; turn off your Web access; disconnect your cell. Yup, easier said than done. So if you need help removing these distractions, let tech come to the rescue!

Some sites function like a nurturing parent—nudging you to get back to business, cheering you on when you're working on your goals. They do this by blocking you from either the entire Internet or specific sites until a predetermined time that you've set. Try weaseling your way out of your commitment and receive a conscience-pricking message like, *"shouldn't you be working?"* Check out AppBlock, StayFocusd and AntiSocial to see if one of these phone apps can be your virtual nurturing parent.

Bookmark sites

"Not now, later." This is the rhetoric that gets so many procrastinators in trouble, yet there are times when those words are spot-on. Let's assume that you're engrossed in an important project. Great! Yet your wandering eye is landing on a breaking story or a tempting link. If you break your concentration, you'll lose your momentum. So, bookmark the site on your computer. After you've finished your work, you'll have plenty of time to visit it.

Track time

Not sure how well you're utilizing your time? Losing track of where all the hours have gone? Consider using a productivity tracking app such as StayFree and RescueTime. Such apps will tell you exactly where your time goes, tracking every Web page you visit, every application you use. It will provide you with time tracking reports and graphs which will likely surprise you, maybe even shock you!

Create to-do lists

With so many things to do, it's easy to forget what you were *going to do*. So, let's hear it for those ubiquitous yellow sticky pads. Now all you have to do is remember where you put them, then remember to look at them. If you're the forgetful type, let *virtual* yellow pads come to the rescue. They're *impossible to misplace or ignore*. They're gadgets that pop up on your phone. For more types of virtual reminders to help you manage your tasks, check out RemembertheMilk and Todoist.

Take notes

You know how busy you can get with stuff to organize, locate and do! Indeed, you've been so busy that the ingenious idea that popped into your head just a few hours ago has popped right out and is now floating around somewhere in outer space. Not good. So, get yourself a cyberspace brain which can remember all your stuff, organize your thoughts and archive your work. Check out Evernote and Scrivener to see how they can enhance your real memory.

Use egg timers

You might be wondering—what's an egg-timer? Before the digital age, people had to use a stand-alone timer to get their eggs boiled the way they wanted them. Nowadays people set egg timers for everything, except eggs. Use the countdown timer on your phone or to find other virtual egg timers, go to e.ggtimer.com or online-stopwatch.com. Set your timer, then work or play until you hear your digital ding—the signal to wrap it up and move on.

These tech tools will prevent you from getting drawn back into the familiar pattern of *"Oh, I'll do it later!"* So, of course, you'll use them! Please don't prove me wrong.

Life After Procrastination

I promised you at the beginning of our journey that I would *not* turn you into a no-fun nerd and I always keep my promises. So now that you're ready to alter your behavior, what will your life be like? Here's what your peers say!

James, a perfectionist: "It took me forever to appreciate how my lofty ambitions were hurting me. I still want to be successful but I've given up the goal of being insanely successful. It's liberating to not always be reaching for unattainable goals. Over-the-top expectations no longer swirl about in my head, making my life one big headache!"

Emma, a dreamer: "I changed from being a head-in-the-clouds dreamer to focusing on what I need to do to make my dreams a reality. I still have big dreams but I know now how I have to hone in on the details, not just the ideas. Some people would roll their eyes when they heard my ideas; now they see I do - not just dream! I'm no longer feeling like a fraud!"

Olivia, a worrier: "I no longer get so worked up over the great, big, overwhelming chore in front of me. From researching a term paper to packing for a trip, I break the chores down into smaller, easier ones that won't send me into a tailspin. Then, one by one, I get those little chores done. I feel as if I've taught myself a secret formula for how to master anything."

Ben, a crisis-maker: "I've always had this crazy idea that I had to wait until crunch time to get my motor running. I never saw what it was doing to me! Now I know I have a choice. I don't need to keep pulling all-nighters. I still need that adrenaline rush, but now I get it from sports, not from self-made crises. I feel great about the person I've become!"

Ethan, a defier: "As a kid, my dad told me I was lazy, stupid and would never amount to anything. So I had good reason to be defensive. But I've changed. I've stopped bucking heads with authority figures and being defensive about criticism. It's paid off big time with my mentor, who has been incredibly helpful to me. And I no longer get snide remarks from friends who were pissed off when I didn't do what I said I'd do."

Ava, a pleaser: "I've stopped trying to get people to like me by always doing what they want. Paying attention to your own ideas might be a no-brainer for others, but for me it's significant progress. I've learned not to drop what I'm doing and always join in with the crowd. Once I put quality time into focusing on myself, I found it easy to choose a career!"

YOU'VE DONE IT!

You've stayed with me all the way to the end. Congrats! Before I bid you farewell, I'd like to summarize a few things you've learned. You now know:

- You need to strive for excellence rather than perfection.
- You need to turn dreams into goals to make them come true.
- You need to break down big, intimidating tasks into smaller tasks that you can do with ease.
- You need to put your executive self in charge more often than your whims and wants.
- You need to reserve your acts of rebellion for what's really worth fighting for.
- You need to focus on what *you* want to achieve not on what others want you to do.
- You need to work hard to achieve your goals; success won't just plop down on your doorstep.
- This one's for you! What's an important idea you now know?

Success happens when you enthusiastically adopt skills to help you become the best version of yourself! Use these skills and the payoff will be an enhanced college experience, elevated self-esteem and enriched career prospects! Excellent payoff, don't you think?

THANK YOU, DEAR READER

A sincere thank you for choosing to read this book. I hope it helped you in many ways - not only to curb your procrastination but also to build up your confidence and self-esteem.

If you found the book helpful, I'd be grateful if you would write a review on Amazon and on your social media sites. It's great for me to hear what was helpful to you. And you'll make a difference when you encourage new readers to discover a valuable resource.

I also appreciate hearing from my readers directly. So don't hesitate to write to me at **LSapadin@DrSapadin.com.**

Or get in touch with me via my websites www.PsychWisdom.com and www.BeatProcrastinationCoach.com.

Wishing you continued success in your college career and beyond.

ACKNOWLEDGMENTS

Though I know a great deal about how to overcome procrastination, it's been many years since I've been a college student. Hence, it was essential for me to get feedback on my manuscript from college students, recent grads and high school students who are headed for college. They have encouraged me with their enthusiasm for the book and suggestions for improving it!

Thanks to Samantha Grant for her creative ideas, sharp insights and never-ending enthusiasm for this book.

Thanks to Eliza Ruston who clearly doesn't procrastinate! She was the first student to read the book and provide me with valuable feedback.

Thanks to Talya Lifshutz whose expertise in everything digital is amazing and was invaluable to me.

Thanks to Danielle Sapadin for her keen observations that helped enhance and enrich this book.

Thanks to Katelynn O'Neill whose enthusiastic feedback and valuable suggestions helped bring life into this book.

Thanks to Santina Leone who strongly suggested that this book needs to be in the hands of high school students, not just college students.

Thanks to Alyssa and Breana Pellicane whose valuable evaluation of the book helped me move the book forward.

Thanks to my colleague Dr. Pauline Wallin who is a tech wiz and friend who notices important details that my eyes glaze over.

Thanks to my husband Dr. Ron Goodrich who enhanced the book by brainstorming with me and providing valuable edits for clearer writing.

Finally, thanks to the students who willingly shared their stories with me. It takes courage and confidence to do so. Respecting your trust in me, I've altered identifying information and merged some experiences of several students' stories into one.

ABOUT THE AUTHOR

Linda Sapadin, Ph.D. is a psychologist and coach who specializes in helping people overcome self-defeating patterns of behavior, especially procrastination. She's been honored with *"Fellow"* status by the American Psychological Association, an indication that her work has had a national impact on the field of psychology.

Her free **e-newsletter PsychWisdom** provides articles on a host of different psychological topics. Subscribe at www.PsychWisdom.com or contact her at **LSapadin@DrSapadin.com.**

Dr. Sapadin is the author of six self-help books that have been published in *the USA, Canada, Japan, Korea, and Australia.* She's appeared on the *Today Show, Good Morning America*, NPR and a host of other TV and radio programs. Her work has been featured in hundreds of newspapers, magazines, podcasts and online publications including *The New York Times, USA Today, The Washington Post, Psychology Today, Men's Health, BBC and WebMD.com*

Dr. Sapadin is a warm, engaging speaker known for the richness and originality of her ideas. Her expertise has been utilized by business and educational organizations, including the S*mithsonian* and the *American Psychological Association.* Pam Weyman, program director of the Smithsonian Associates, said Dr. Sapadin is an example of "the best standard of instructors at the Smithsonian, an institution that seeks out only the most qualified in their field."

Dr. Sapadin's website **www.BeatProcrastinationCoach.com** describes her coaching services. It also has inspirational quotes for the reader to pursue. Her website **www.PsychWisdom.com** contains informative articles for readers, such as *Battle of the Brain - Can People Really Change? - Failure to Launch Syndrome - Resolutions You Might Actually Keep* - and many more!

Additional Books by DR. SAPADIN

How to Beat Procrastination in the Digital Age: *6 Change Programs for 6 Personality Styles.* PsychWisdom Publishing, 2012.

Procrastination Busting Strategies for Perfectionists. Kindle Book. PsychWisdom Publishing, 2013.

Master Your Fears: *How to Triumph Over Your Worries and Get On With Your Life.* John Wiley, 2004. Also published in Korea.

Now I Get It! *Totally Sensational Advice for Living and Loving.* A collection of empowering and entertaining columns on expanding personal growth. Outskirts Press, 2007. Inkstone Press (Australia), 2008.

How to Beat Procrastination and Make the Grade: *The 6 Styles of Procrastination and How Students Can Overcome Them.* Penguin, 1999.

It's About Time! *The 6 Styles of Procrastination and How to Overcome Them.* Viking and Penguin, 1996. Also published in Japan.